We are living in a time of a gre
and humanity as a whole. There
in the paradigms and conscious

izing a Freedom that they'd always possessed, and yet didn't know. More and
more are realizing a unifying Source that connects all of creation.

Love.

This Source is Love.

Seeing that God is Love, and God was most fully represented by Jesus, both
human and Divine—as a self-revelation of Love—changes everything.

Jamal Jivanjee adds his beautiful expression to a growing chorus of voices
who are learning to *be* loved, and *to* love... free. This book will open your eyes
and heart to a world that is here and coming—a Kingdom in which only Love
remains—and the courage and trust to live in this New World...now.

Love is within, and is expressed in relationship—all relationships. You will be
challenged, yet encouraged, and filled with hope as you wrestle with Jamal's
vision of Love through relationships of every kind.

Throughout my own participation in this great transformation, I have been
challenged and have come to change my mindset about so much. I've
learned to trust what I see and hear and think along the lines of Jesus'
encouragement of "you'll know them by their fruit." If something causes
me to see a smaller God (or to feel worse about myself and others, or
exclude, etc.) then the fruit tells me that is not something to trust. If, however, something causes me to see a bigger God, to feel more loved, to love
all others more, and to become more inclusive, hopeful, and merciful... well,
then that is fruit I can trust.

Such is the message of *Free to Love*.

(BRANDON CHASE, AUTHOR AND BLOGGER, BRANDONCHASE.NET)

There is a revolution of love going on in the world today, yet some Christians hold back from joining this revolution because we fear the appearance of improper relationships with other people—especially with people of the opposite sex. In his book, *Free to Love*, Jamal Jivanjee shows that when Jesus called us to love one another and to experience the oneness of relational love, Jesus wasn't just referring to the oneness of marital love, but to something much deeper. Yes, this oneness can be experienced in a marriage relationship, but it can (and should) also be experienced in relationships outside of marriage. Does this sound 'dangerous'? Yes. But since when is love ever safe? If we hold back from the love that Jesus invites us into with other people, we will never truly experience the oneness-love of the Triune God. No longer live with your fear to love. Instead, read this book and discover that in Jesus, you are *Free to Love*.

(JEREMY MYERS, AUTHOR AND BIBLE TEACHER, REDEEMINGGOD.COM)

Free to Love sizzles with brave energy! Jamal artfully weaves a compelling short story through a provocative call to deeply love others. His words challenge me to engage in relationships beyond our culture's man-made boundaries. I am excited to recommend *Free to Love* to those who desire to follow Christ's command to 'love one another' more fully.

(BRIANNA L. GEORGE, SPEAKER AND WRITER, UNVEILEDANDREVEALED.COM)

FREE TO LOVE

HOW ONENESS TRANSCENDS MARRIAGE AND SINGLENESS

JAMAL JIVANJEE

First Edition

Cover design and layout by Rafael Polendo (polendo.net)
Cover photo by alfonsodetomas (photodune.com)

ISBN 978-0-9913345-6-8

This volume is printed on acid free paper and meets ANSI Z39.48 standards.

Printed in the United States of America

Published by Quoir
Orange, California

www.quoir.com

DEDICATION

This book is dedicated to my daughter.

Although we have had trouble in the world, be encouraged, we have overcome the world. We stand on the shores of an entirely new land.

TABLE OF CONTENTS

ACKNOWLEDGEMENTS

Where do I begin? There are no words adequate enough to thank all those who have contributed to the writing and publication of this project. To do so would require another book to be written. As I've wrestled over the implications of this paradigm for the last several years, I've not been alone on this journey. Many have walked this road with me, and for that, I'm beyond grateful.

First, I'd like to thank my family who have been a part of a journey they didn't necessarily ask to be a part of. I'd like to thank my parents for their unconditional acceptance during each season of my life. The arrows that have pierced my heart have also pierced theirs. I'd also like to thank Brandie and Jessica for their sacrifice. This journey has been very costly for them in ways that many will never know.

I'd like to thank the members of our focus group (Rafael Polendo, Barrett Johnson, Jennifer Cowles, Brandon Chase, Franklin Reagan, Rose Glasser, Pamela Spock, and Diya Wahi) for their careful review of the manuscript. The analysis and insight they provided is worth more than gold.

To Rafael Polendo and the team at Quoir, words seem inadequate to express the magnitude of my thanks. A few years ago before Quoir was born, Rafael spoke what I know to be divine words to me about writing. Little did we know then, this particular book would be the fruit of that encouragement. Quoir's vision of many voices proclaiming one message is demonstrated through this book's existence. Because the subject matter of this book carries a high risk of being misunderstood, it was not a light decision for Quoir to support this work. Most publishers would not touch a book that carries such risk. I consider Quoir to be a company that truly gives a voice to the growing assembly of marginalized voices beyond the walls of religion. I will forever be grateful for the price they have paid to publish this book. It will not be forgotten.

I owe a debt of gratitude to the late Jay Ferris for his belief in me and for his unashamed expression of love for me in the short time we knew one another on this earth. What he imparted to me has made the writing of this book possible. He showed me that we truly are lovers in training and that there is no shame in learning to love like God.

On more of a personal note, I'd like to thank Pamela Spock, Nischelle Reagan, Jessica Sagri, and Tara Thomas (a.k.a. The Guild) for their unwavering support and friendship when all others fell away. They never lost sight of me. They never drew back, even when it was costly. Not once. The proverbs speak of a friend that "sticks closer than a brother", and I have found the friendship of these precious sisters to be the very closest. I am eternally grateful for the gift of their presence in my life. This book could not have been written without them.

Lastly, I am grateful for the Son of Love Himself for all that He has chosen to reveal to me of His heart. Thank you for trusting me with your most precious desire—the desire for oneness.

–Jamal

"THE TWO MOST IMPORTANT DAYS IN YOUR LIFE ARE THE DAY YOU ARE BORN AND THE DAY YOU FIND OUT WHY."

(MARK TWAIN)

CHAPTER 1
ONCE UPON A TIME

Many years ago, there was a man who had it all. One who was the offspring of pure love. He was the crown of creation, and the delight of Abba's heart. He was given a beautiful and secure place to live, and all the food he could possibly desire. Not only did this man have all the material possessions he needed, he also had access to true companionship; a companionship that most of humanity could hardly dream of. This man walked with God. Face to face.

Like his creator, this man was also a living community as well. In order to express the full image and likeness of God, this man had a woman inside of him. The two, male and female, were really one person. They lacked nothing. Like the rest of creation, humanity was declared to be good.

There was a problem, however. This man eventually began to feel utterly alone, and that wasn't good.[1]

When the man became lonely, this grieved God's heart as a parent. God had given birth to humanity to share love and union with them, never loneliness and isolation. Loneliness and isolation is a darkness that is foreign to the light and life of God. God would give him a picture of the union he was created for, yet even that gift would not be enough to alleviate his suffering from the illusion.

That picture is marriage.

The woman, who was already in him, was taken out of him and presented to him as a picture of the community and union they already possessed. Unfortunately, the demands of a lie can never be satisfied. The man was not able to receive the gift of the woman as the expression of the community and union they already possessed. It wasn't long before this sense of inadequacy and lack permeated their beings like cancer. This led to their decision to turn away from the source of light and life and into the darkness of the lie of separation and lack.

As you may know, I'm speaking of Adam and Eve. As the first standard bearers of humanity, their sickness and sadness from the lie infected all of their offspring down to you and I. The picture of *marriage* could only go so far. Their condition led to a breakdown between the genders. In their quest to satisfy their longing for union and significance, men would dominate and exploit women, and the women would cling to and seek to acquire from men. The relationship between male and female was largely understood in this context until a pivotal point in human history.

The second *Adam,* Jesus Christ, was born into this realm.

Until Christ came, marriage was also understood in this context. Although marriage was always meant to be a picture pointing back to a greater reality, marriage began to be seen as the highest form of human intimacy and connection. When Christ revealed the ultimate image and expression of God and destroyed the power of the lie of separation and lack, the dynamic of human existence and relational community radically changed. For the first time in history, the reality that marriage pointed to began to come into view.

This reality is oneness.

In the new covenant inaugurated by Jesus Christ, true love has been perfectly and fully revealed through Him. God is love, and love gave birth to the cosmos. In order for love to be fully known, however, something called *oneness* must be illuminated and put on display to the cosmos through humanity. The problem is, oneness has been hidden behind an idol that was never meant to be an idol.

That idol is marriage.

Lies are being told about marriage by the same paradigm that claims to uphold and cherish it. We may think idols refer to small gold or silver figurines, but idolatry generally refers to anything we treat as "ultimate". For millennia, we have made an idol of marriage: treating a good thing as ultimate, and in doing so we have distorted its meaning. In the name of upholding and cherishing marriage, we have told lies about it because we have elevated a good thing into an ultimate thing. As a result, the Lord's purpose for all creation is regularly assaulted in the name of honoring love and marriage.

The advance of Jesus' new kingdom into the world has illuminated our understanding and practice of just about everything. The heart of the Lord regarding the pictures or shadows provided to us in the Old Covenant take on a proper function in light of the new reality revealed in the new covenant. For example, the Sabbath as a day of rest in the Old Covenant, points to the greater reality of a lifestyle of rest in the New. This is one example among many we could talk about. The shadows of the old were meant to point to the reality of the new. *It's fabulous news indeed.*

Yet, so many are afraid to talk about how the most glorious shine of marriage is now being outshone by a new reality.

Yes, I said *outshone*. Anytime a greater expression comes into view, the brighter light outshines the lesser light. For many of us, the thought of marriage being eclipsed by a greater light is deeply troubling. This is nothing new. Throughout church history there has been an unfortunate propensity to revert back to the types and shadows of Christ, overshadowing the very reality they were designed to reveal.

Unfortunately, in absence of this revelation, a religious system began to form that preferred the types and shadows of Christ than the present reality of Christ Himself. An Old Covenant religious system began to form using New Testament terminology. Glorious realities like the incarnation and resurrection were reduced to 'sacred' holy days, remembered a couple of times a year.

No, this isn't a book about the advent of days like Christmas and Easter. I'm simply attempting to shed some light on the roots of something a bit more systemic in nature. This is especially true in regards to marriage. My heartfelt desire in writing this book is two fold:

- First, to identify and tear down commonly held beliefs about marriage that have made it into an idol it was never meant to be.

- Second, that we would gain a fresh vision of oneness that is in harmony with the New Covenant.

I need to be honest with you, however. If you decide to read further, you may feel defensive, or even offended. This book may also cause you to struggle. This struggle may be within you, within your household, and within your community of relationships. This book may even bring out deep divisions between you and significant others. That's okay: I am intimately familiar with this struggle.

I want you to know these pages have not been written lightly. This book has been in the making for the last twenty years. No, not the writing specifically, but the revelations and the experience. What I will share with you in this book has cost me dearly. It has cost me everything from some of my closest relationships, down to even my very own marriage. Nothing warranted these losses on my part, and my heart remains open and hopeful for the day reconciliation will occur. Because I have paid dearly for the things you will read in this book, however, I believe I am uniquely qualified to write this book. I have a friend who says "love costs us everything, but takes very little." I have discovered that to be true. The things you will read in these pages have been worth every tear, every wound, every misunderstanding, every sleepless night, and even the temporary loss of my most treasured relationships. What you will read in this book has given birth to the purest, most Christ centered relationships I've ever had. I am at rest knowing the new, glorious kingdom that has come into view as a result of this struggle is in harmony with the heart of our Lord. Although I have been profoundly sad and have shed countless tears, I am not sad anymore.

I am profoundly hopeful.

As we embark on this journey, I would ask you to read with an open mind. We all have natural yes but, or what about questions as we read, but I would ask you to bear with me and suspend judgment until the end. Pray that you would see what you are supposed to see regardless of how different it may seem to all you have known, experienced, or been taught.

What you will read in these pages is for you personally, whether you're married or single. Again, as the idol of marriage is torn down and *oneness* comes into view, I believe we will begin to see an entirely new world. The more we come into alignment with this new world of love, the more needless suffering and lovesickness will dissipate in every area of our lives. For some, this alignment will lead to deep emotional healing and the end of cycles of depression and anxiety. For others, I envision a more physical healing like the opening of once barren wombs. *It moves me to tears just thinking about it.*

It is not an accident or coincidence you are reading this. I believe you've been chosen to discover a whole new world, and it is truly an honor to take this journey with you.

"JESUS IS OPENING UP TO THEM A WHOLE NEW WORLD. IT IS THE WORLD OF THE FATHER IN WHICH HIS BREATH IS THE NEW MIMESIS OF SELF-GIVING LOVE, RATHER THAN FEARFUL RIVALRY."

(ANDRE RABE)

CHAPTER 2
A LADDER OR A CIRCLE?

As I was in the midst of writing this book, a friend and I were having lunch with a college aged student when she asked about the subject of this book. I told her it was a book that would explore rethinking marriage and relationships in light of the new kingdom that has come to the earth. As one who was actively looking to find that someone special to marry, she asked me what advice I could give her about marriage.

I told her about the glorious possibility of loving others deeply as family and experiencing oneness with others as a remedy to the human sickness of loneliness regardless of gender, ethnicity, or any other fleshly distinction. I reminded her about Jesus' prayer for us to experience the same kind of relational oneness with one another that He has with His Father. I told her this was possible both within marriage, and also with those we are not married to. Sometimes the longing we interpret as a desire for marriage is really a longing for intimacy and acceptance that we can have in a multitude of new kingdom relationships. Contrary to popular opinion, intimacy is not necessarily synonymous with romance and sexual intercourse. She became quiet. I could tell she was thinking. Then she said this:

"That's a nice concept, but I'm not sure how I feel about the possibility of my future husband having close relationships with other women.

As his wife, it's important for him to put me first, and for me to put him first."

If I had a dime for every time this objection was used to justify the hierarchical status quo view of marriage and relationships, I'd be a millionaire. It's something said so often it just sounds true; but is it really? When people say their spouse should come 'first', what are they really saying? I think it's revealing of something much deeper. It reveals the grid through which we see everything: one of competition, rather than harmony.

COMPETITION

In the old world, everything is viewed through the lens of competition, rivalry, and hierarchy. Relationships are no exception. Many view relationships as rungs or steps on a ladder with the top being the most intimate and close, and the bottom being the least. The goal is to climb the ladder and get to the top. The rungs closest to one another are in the most competition.

In most evangelical or religious ideas of marriage and relationships, it is thought that marriage is the top rung on the relational ladder, with a significant gap between marriage and the rest of the rungs of relationship. This 'gap' will keep the other 'rungs' far down the relational ladder, safe from competing with the top placed rung occupied by the spouse. If any other 'rungs' get close to the top rung, the marriage is in danger of being compromised.

HARMONY

In the new kingdom of God, competition, rivalry, and hierarchy are foreign because they are foreign to the nature of love. God is love, and competition, rivalry, and hierarchy are foreign to His nature. In the kingdom of God, there is no lack; therefore there is no need to strive for survival utilizing those tools. Putting one family member 'above' another family member in the family of God doesn't make sense because God doesn't rank His love for some above or below others. Because the source of love is infinite, the fullness or uniqueness of His love for me isn't compromised by the fullness and uniqueness of His love for you.

My friend Sarah's grandfather passed away a few years ago. Her grandfather loved her immensely, and unconditionally. When we talk about her grandfather, I can see the love he lavished on her by the glow and smile that lights up her face and the tears that fill her eyes. His love for her radically altered her life.

As I have met and spent time with Sarah's siblings and cousins, it's apparent to me all the grandkids felt this way about their grandfather. They all seemed to have a unique and full relationship with him, too. In one conversation between Sarah and her cousin, her cousin talked about how much she missed her grandfather. She reminisced about the weekly calls she received from her grandfather, and how much they meant to her. After the conversation, my friend looked at me with a look of delight and said, *"he used to call me every week, too!"*

Because Sarah understood the unique nature of her grandfather's love for her, hearing of his love for the other grandkids didn't trouble her at all. It simply deepened her appreciation for how loving a man her grandfather is. He didn't need to place her above the other grandkids for her to know and celebrate the uniqueness of their relationship. God's love for us is the same.

No one has the unique relationship you have with our heavenly Daddy. It is truly one of a kind. Thankfully, He doesn't have to put any of us second or third to preserve the sacred uniqueness of the relationship He has with you. In His love and kingdom, we're all first. I'm convinced the kingdom of God is more like a circle of relationships joined together in the harmonious dance of the trinity, not a hierarchy of relationships placed as rungs on a ladder with some being above and below others.

In a marriage awakened to the new kingdom, marriage fits into this harmonious circle of relationships safe and secure. No competition and hierarchy is needed to protect and preserve the uniqueness and sacredness of the marital relationship that stands alone on its own right. We'll touch on that later in the book. With that said, however, I'd like to tell you a bit more about my journey to find a bride. A heavenly bride.

"LOVE DEEPLY, WHEREVER YOU ARE, WITH WHOM YOU ARE. START WITH YOURSELF, BECAUSE THAT IS WHERE GOD IS, AND HAS ALWAYS BEEN. THEN, YOU'LL BEGIN TO SEE GOD IN ALL OTHERS TOO, AND LOVE THEM THE SAME WAY."

(BRANDON CHASE)

CHAPTER 3
LOOKING FOR A HEAVENLY BRIDE

I've been blogging full time since 2011. I never anticipated becoming a blogger, but then again, I never anticipated most of the things I've encountered in life. In my blogging career, I've written extensively about something I am passionate about: the church. For most of my adult life, I've been passionate about the bride of Christ. I have always wanted to discover the essence of the church Jesus envisioned, and I was utterly disillusioned with all that I experienced as 'church'. I thought I could create the church I longed for, the church I had so often read about in the New Testament. So, I went to a university and earned a degree in religion with a concentration in Pastoral studies. Shortly after college, I recruited a staff, raised some money, and planted a church.

After spending four years as a local church Pastor, I discovered I was building the very thing I said I wasn't going to build, and decided I needed to step back a bit. I read a lot of stories about the church as it existed beyond the western context, and I sensed the need to see those communities for myself. As a result, I put together a team of about twelve people with a similar desire and we traveled the world. We visited people and communities in places like the Middle East, China, Tibet, Nepal and India. The church communities we visited in some of those places were

underground and fiercely persecuted. Many of my western institutional paradigms of church and community were shattered by
my experience. After that trip, I knew I couldn't continue my
current career in the clergy, so I stepped down from my position
in the religious institution I had built.

It didn't take long before I discovered there were many others who were also rethinking 'church' structure and essence. I
discovered authors who had written about the Pagan origins of
institutional religion as an explanation as to why church in the
Western world looked so different than the church recorded in
the New Testament.[2] It was music to my ears. Finally, there were
others who were putting words to things awaking in my heart.
Other books followed about rethinking the church, and also
about the glories and hardships of organic church life.[3]

The premise was beautiful. Christ is head of the church, not
a select person or group of people (clergy), and each member
had the right to express Christ through word or deed when the
church had its meetings (priesthood of all believers). Again, it all
seemed to be scratching the itch for New Testament community
I had. I hadn't been this excited in a long time.

I was told my best course of action was to join a group that
had been planted by people who had experience in this kind
of life. We were told to discover and kill all our agendas, die to
self, detox from all our previously held ideas, and eventually we
would begin to experience New Testament church life. That's
exactly what I did for the next few years.

I learned a lot during this season. We experienced weekly
meetings in which everyone had a role to play, not just a select
few on a stage that was typical of institutional churches we had
all come out of. We were also instructed on how to make decisions by consensus and follow Christ's leading as head of the

church. There were systems and activities put in place to help us achieve these community goals.

In the beginning, things were rich and exciting. Instead of simply attending events and meetings the way many of us had in more institutional forms of church, some seemed truly interested in relating to one another and sharing the life of Christ with one another in a more 'organic' way. Others, however, seemed content to limit their participation and involvement to the weekly house church meeting.

The community had been taught to look for and see expressions of Christ in nature, movies, music, scripture, food and drink, etc. Unfortunately, the one place where many seemed to struggle to see and relate to Christ the most is in the place where He fully dwells: other people. There are several reasons relating to Christ in people was so difficult. These reasons will hopefully become clear to you as you move forward in the book.

While the indwelling life of Christ was often spoken of in theory among the group as a whole, close personal relationships fueled by love often seemed foreign. Individuals loving one another necessitate the existence of authentic relationships in which people can freely relate to one another. This was intimidating to many due to the traditional relational and marital paradigms through which we had been accustomed to operate.

After a while, frustration began to set in. A preoccupation with *dying to self* and *denying the desires of self* became the focus in the name of embracing the cross. Although this seemed noble on the surface, it was simply a fear-based preoccupation with self in reality. The effect on relationships was chilling, as love is others focused by nature. The weekly meetings became dry and routine. Many others felt the group was not close enough, so as a result, group events were planned outside the formal church meetings. Schedules were filled with group camping outings, group getaways, early morning coffee gatherings, and dinners thinking this would fix the relational problem. It didn't. The more restless people became, the more the dominant personalities in the group would demand the group *die* to their own agendas and get in line with the original vision. Fear of becoming an agent of dissension and disunity was used to keep others from acknowledging their frustration. As you can imagine, things became toxic quickly.

I began to learn this problem wasn't unique to the *organic* church I was a part of, this was a problem in many groups that were attempting to experience authentic church life in a natural/organic way. Ironically, the lack of significant deep relationships and busyness with group meetings and activities were the same reasons why many left the institutional religious system in the first place. Many have asked me why this cycle keeps repeating itself. As a blogger who writes about authentic New Testament community, I regularly receive questions about how to find or create an authentic *organic* church. Most people are looking for a method or system to put into place. The first thing I tell folks is this...

We can't create the church because the church has already been created.

We simply get the privilege of recognizing what the Lord is already putting together. Most respond by telling me they don't see the Lord putting together an authentic community in their area, and they feel alone as a result. There is a reason people feel this way, and it's not because the Lord isn't building His church there.

Contrary to the opinion of some in organic church circles, God doesn't lack anything. Many think they need to build the Lord's house because He is homeless. I've heard this taught often. David, the former king of ancient Israel, also felt this way and He offered to build God's house. God responded by asking David how he could possibly build a house big enough to contain Him. It's laughable. God has built us a house, actually. His name is Jesus, and we're a part of the fabric of this house already.

*Jesus said He would build His church, but as living stones of this dwelling, He asked us to **love** one another in the same way He loved others.*

He prayed that we would experience oneness with one another in the same way He and His Father experienced oneness together.

He said it would be our love for one another that would show the world His nature. This looks like relationship that is deep, intimate, and that crosses all religious and social boundaries erected by fear and the lie of lack dating back to the garden.[4] While I am thankful for what has been written about rethinking mission, rethinking theology, and rethinking church structure, rethinking what it means to have intimate relationships and communication from that perspective is desperately needed today.

Ultimately, the church is a group of people held together by divine, relational love. This love is the substance of Christ, the new wine. Thankfully, we are full of this new wine because we have the fullness of indwelling love dwelling within (Col. 1:27). This love is unlike anything the world knows, and it cannot be understood through old paradigms and systems. Tremendous upheaval will be the result. This is precisely why Jesus said we couldn't put new wine into old wineskins.[5] If that occurs, the wineskin will explode and the new wine will be wasted. I have seen this occur and I have experienced this personally in my own journey. It is tremendously painful, and there is always a lot of unnecessary collateral damage.

True relational love is opposed by the religious paradigms of this world. In my experience both in traditional and non-traditional religious systems, forging intimate relationships remain challenging despite desperate attempts to manufacture close community through group events, programs, and even participatory meetings in living rooms. Intimate relationships in these environments are not only foreign; they are often seen with suspicion and opposed. Again, the fear of close personal relationships are detrimental to truly seeing and experiencing Christ considering the fact it is our love for one another that makes Christ visible on the earth.

When blog readers contact me regarding their frustration with not being able to find authentic community, or when they ask me how to start or create authentic church community, they are usually not impressed with my response. I often ask them if there is anyone they are currently attracted to. This usually gets their attention. I ask them if there is anyone in their circle they feel a deep longing to connect with or to get to know better. This question may seem bizarre or off topic. It's really not. Finding community has to begin with seeing the people that are already around us.

It's easy to become so busy trying to find, create, or even to maintain a group that we miss seeing actual people. If we can't see and delight in the people in our daily lives that we rub shoulders with, how can we have relationship with them?

Every life exists at the cellular level. As cells function and relate to one another, you have the makings of a body. Cells sharing life together are like relationships. Regardless if there are just a few cells, or many, life is sustained and experienced at the cellular level. The same is true for church life. The life and love of Christ is experienced and shared at the relational, one to one level. Although we may interact and participate in larger groups, we have relationship with specific people, not entities or groups.

Apart from real relationships knit together in love, everything else is simply theory and form.

When people think of *church,* some think of a physical location where a preprogrammed service is performed by a select few on a stage. Others may think of a group gathered in a specific location for a participatory meeting of sorts. In reality, the church Jesus builds isn't a weekly performance by a select few, nor is the kingdom of God a preoccupation with participatory meetings in living rooms. The bride of Christ is people built together in intimate relationships through love.

I'm not a doctor, but I've heard one of the first things cancer does is it prevents cells from communicating (relating) to one another. This allows the cancer-ridden cell to be completely overtaken by the cancer without being affected by the other healthy cells that are filled with life. In the same way, false mindsets and paradigms (be they religious misconceptions of God and humanity, false understandings of church, or relational fears) are like cancer. They prevent people from seeing one another with delight, from communicating and receiving life from each other, and from entering into intimate relationships.

Jesus radically redefined what it means to be a friend. Although Jesus knew and interacted with lots of people, He had few friends. At the end of His life, Jesus called His disciples friends because He said He was able to share *everything* with them. The essence of His life was everything the Father gave Him (John 15:15). That's pretty intimate, if you ask me. He saved the term *friend* for the few with whom He walked in relational oneness. It was through these intimate relationships that He experienced a true-shared life community.

This might sound shocking, but I'm convinced it would do us well to stop trying to figure out how to find and create *church* and instead to learn what it means to see, delight, know, serve, and deeply love one another through relationship. This is where oneness will be found. After all, Jesus never asked us to build His church, but He did ask us to love one another.[6] Maybe when we discover how to intimately relate to and love one another from the infinite reservoir of love within us, we'll discover what He's been building. I've gotten a glimpse myself, and it's so beautiful, it's *scandalous*.

THE DAY OF LOVE

The stirring in my spirit became impossible to ignore. The day was fast approaching and I knew a new chapter was beginning. Everything was going to change. All my days had prepared me for this. The wellspring of water within was becoming more like a geyser. Father spoke of this day long ago, and now it was finally upon me.

The thought of telling mother brought a sense of nauseous dread. How could I? I knew she dreaded this day, and I think I felt her dread in my own body. When I finally broke the news, she already knew. I guess a mother always knows. I watched as the sorrow filled her eyes. She remembered the words spoken to her when I was brought to the temple just days after my birth. She had been expecting the time to come when her love for me would painfully pierce her own soul. I could see, from the look in her eyes, that time had come.

As I took to the dusty road on my journey, Father filled me with a great sense of expectation. I hadn't seen John in years, and I knew my Father had something special for me there. The peace and anticipation in my spirit seemed to grow with each mile. When I finally reached the summit overlooking the Jordan, my heart melted. All those precious people streaming out into the desert, desperate for the new kingdom he had been announcing. Father had something for me there, with John, and I couldn't get down the summit fast enough to walk into this new chapter. This is why I was born.

As John's arms lifted me from the water, Father spoke something that comforted me more than I can express with words. Although mother tried to protect me from the talk about my origins, I knew what so many thought about me. I could tell by the way they looked at her. The speculation about who my father was always seemed to come up in someone's conversation. Although I knew what was true, it still hurt to hear the lies. To hear Father claim me and speak of His love and pleasure of me so publicly was deeply healing to me. I treasured it in my heart, and I knew it would be the foundation from which I would passionately love others.

Those words from my Father were tested quickly. In the desert, my identity was assaulted in a new way. I had to hang on to those words with my very life. They sustained me when I was alone. When my time of solitude was over, however, I experienced a desire that was also new to me. This desire would prepare me to share in some of my Father's greatest gifts to which He was sending me.

The time of love had come. I desired to give the best of me away. I desired to feast from the life and light of the anointed ones my Father would give me. One by one, I met them, and one by one, we began to walk together. Although I could spend a lifetime telling you about each one of those precious ones, there is one in particular that I'd like to talk to you about…

CHAPTER 4
VANISHING CONVERSATIONS

Recently, as I was driving through a major city here in the States, I decided to surf through the radio dial. I stumbled upon a sermon from a well-known mega-church pastor in the city where I was driving, so I figured I would listen in for a bit. He was talking about *the place of worship,* and where that place is. I decided to listen to what he had to say. As I listened, my heart sank.

This well respected doctor of theology described the place of worship, in the Old Testament, as the temple in Jerusalem. It was the place where people would bring their tithes/offerings, and their sacrifices. He went on to say the *place* of worship in the new covenant is the local church. Unfortunately, he described the local church in the exact same way he described the Old Testament temple...as a *place.* He described it as a place where people hold a religious service or meeting once a week. While this is a common understanding within institutional Christianity that I was well aware of, something astounding caught my attention.

A monumental conversation had vanished.

Some conversations are game changers. Some conversations are so monumental, life after the conversation is radically different from life before the conversation. Jesus had a truly monumental conversation with the Samaritan woman recorded in

John 4 about worship that changed everything.[7] Our understanding of worship, and the place of worship, radically changed after this conversation. Trying to grasp worship without this conversation is impossible.

At the beginning of the conversation, the Samaritan woman understood worship in the way most people at that time understood it; as a function to be performed in a specific place, in a specific building, at a specific time. Jesus completely blew her paradigm out of the water, however, when He told her a new era of worship was dawning.

Worship would no longer be confined to a specific place, a specific time, or a specific location. Worship would now be lived out in the realm of spirit and reality (truth). True worship would transcend beyond the borders of location and time, as God is spirit. He is not limited by the distinctions of space and time. Without this conversation between Jesus and the Samaritan woman, worship would still be understood as a shadow of what it truly is. If I were an enemy of true worship, I would seek to erase that monumental conversation and keep us living in the shadows. That is indeed what has happened as evidenced by the sermon I heard on the radio that day.

Jesus' paradigm shifting conversation about worship with the Samaritan woman isn't the only conversation that has vanished, unfortunately. There is a paradigm shifting and reality altering conversation about *marriage* that seems to have also gone missing. The results of this missing conversation have been just as devastating, keeping us stuck in the shadows. There is a reason for this. Like Jesus' conversation about worship, this conversation about marriage has the potential to awaken us to a new reality that has direct implications to the purpose of God on the earth.

SOMETHING DEEPER THAN RELIGION AND CULTURE

A few years back, when I took my world trip with a team to back pack around the world discovering people and cultures outside of our western paradigm, it was truly a life changing experience. Whether we were in North America, Europe, Africa, the Middle East, or Asia, what surprised me the most was how much we all have in common. This is especially true in light of all the things that seemingly keep humanity separated from each other. What we have in common must go deeper than all the things that divide us like religion, cultural traditions, economics, security needs, or ethnicity. Since that's a lot to overcome, what we have in common must point to the essence of our humanity.

Although ceremonies and religious traditions differ in different places, weddings exist and are celebrated everywhere I have traveled in the world. Every culture values and celebrates marriage in some form or fashion. To my knowledge, there isn't a culture that doesn't. This is fascinating to me. It points to a deep-seated longing in humanity.

It's not good for us to be alone.

Remember Adam's longing? Remember the picture?

Marriage.

Being joined together as one with another. This is a common human longing that transcends everything else. It's actually fundamental to our humanity. We were not made to be alone. We were made for oneness.

So, that's it right? Our deep seated need of oneness was demonstrated through marriage, right? That's the common sentiment of most. Pop culture communicates this. Religion enshrines it. But, is there more to the story? Yes! In order to discover the rest of the story, however, we'll have to revisit a conversation that has largely been kept hidden from you.

DID YOU REALLY JUST SAY THAT?

Several years ago, I was speaking to a group of people in college and their early twenties. The topic was relationships, so many of the people came to hear the talk with quite a bit of anticipation. They wanted insight about how to know or discern God's will regarding whether or not their significant other was *the one* for them. They also wanted to know how to improve upon their romantic and marital relationships. They were shocked when I told them this:

"It's better to be single."

The looks on their faces spoke volumes. I think I even heard a few gasps. They were waiting for the punch line. It never came. I saw looks of bewilderment, confusion, offense, and disbelief. The glances of many of them went to my wife who was sitting in the congregation. How could I, as a married man, say that publicly? I later learned several people present in the audience for that talk began to be concerned I had a low view of marriage and that I was speaking out of discontentment in my own marriage. It didn't seem to matter I was sharing a conversation Paul was having with the church community at Corinth. It was easier to dismiss me as a messenger than Paul.

The church community in Corinth had sent Paul a letter about issues they were having concerning marital relationships and sexual immorality. The letter of 1 Corinthians was Paul's response to them. The particular view Paul was refuting in 1 Corinthians 7 was their assertion that maybe it was better for people (including married people) *not* to have sex at all (7:1). This was due to the influence of dualistic views of the body as a result of gnostic ideas.

He told them that, in light of the sexual immorality that had been occurring, married people should not deprive their spouse's sexual needs. Sexual immorality was occurring and spouses relating sexually were a safe guard against sexual immorality. In the midst of saying that, however, he isn't shy about letting them know how he really feels about this advice. This statement is quite stunning:

"I say this as a concession, not as a command. I wish that all of you were as I am (single). But each of you has your own gift from God; one has this gift, another has that." **(1 COR. 7:6-7, NIV)**

Can you believe Paul actually said he is making a concession in his heart when he tells spouses to be sexually intimate so they won't be tempted with illicit sexual desire? Having sex out of the fear of potential infidelity is a behavior that falls short of the highest motivations of love. This is not the norm in the kingdom of God. Paul does not hide the fact that if he could have his way, everyone would have the *gift* of being single like he is.[8] Can you believe he saw singleness as a *gift* to be wished on everyone? Can you believe he viewed the typical marital relationship as a *concession?*

Are you mad yet? In case you think I'm reading too much into this, consider what he says next:

"Now to the unmarried and to the widows I say: it is good for them to stay unmarried, as I do." **(1 COR. 7:8, NIV)**

As you can imagine, this conversation from Paul wasn't welcome news to the mostly single, college aged Christians who came out with great anticipation to hear me talk about relationships. This seemed like really bad news to them. For most, it was simply too devastating to consider. How could it be good for anyone to stay single? The single folks listening to me talk that night knew what singleness was like. They were living in it, and they were longing for so much more. They desired what we all do: *oneness.* Oneness is the deepest longing of our being.

They saw Paul's advice to remain single as an albatross keeping them confined in their loneliness. Although Paul said it was *good* for them to stay unmarried, they didn't really believe that. As a matter of fact, I don't know many people who would readily admit that it's good for people to stay unmarried. That's why an expectation is put on people to be married by a certain age. Deep down, we all know we were made for oneness. We long for oneness, but are *oneness* and *marriage* inseparable? Are they the same thing? That's the million-dollar question. Before we address that, however, we need a closer glimpse of what oneness is.

"THE FATHER AND I ARE ONE."

(JESUS CHRIST, NLT)

CHAPTER 5
VERTICAL ONENESS

Although we cannot recall our time in the womb as adults, much happened during that time that shaped and gave us some context into the world in which we were born. Another woman cannot satisfy the longing of a newborn baby like its mother. Although others may hold the child immediately after birth, the child inherently knows the moment they are being held by their mother despite having never seen her face. The child is already intimately connected to her because of their connection in the womb. The bond between mother and child is unmatched and life-long. As a matter of fact, studies have shown the cry of a newborn baby caries a rhythm and pitch that matches the rhythm and pitch of the mother's voice. A newborn baby and its mother are a fascinating picture of oneness.

Twins are also fascinating to me. I'm intrigued by the fact that a twin is together with their sibling from the very beginning. They begin to grow and develop side by side in the same inner chamber of the mother. Some twins even share the same placenta and food supply. The connection that twins have, beginning in the womb, runs quite deep. Deeper than conscious memory even. It should be no surprise to know many twins have experienced a connection that baffles logic and rational explanation. Many times, when one twin is experiencing deep pain or joy, the other is aware of their twin and often experiences the same symptoms. This can occur even among twins that have been separated over great time and distances; unaware of the specific circumstances that may be affecting the other.

These are just a couple of examples that illustrate that a greater reality of connection can exist that transcends natural explanation. The scriptures tell us the natural world is filled with pictures that point to greater heavenly realities. If such stunning examples of oneness exist in our natural world, how much greater is the reality that exists in the spiritual?

We get a fascinating picture of this oneness when we look at the life of Jesus and the connection He experienced with His Father. Jesus prayed we would experience the exact same oneness with one another that He experiences with His Father.[9] So before we jump into the discussion of the nature of oneness we can experience between one another (horizontal oneness), we want to catch a glimpse of the oneness Jesus enjoyed with His Father.

The scriptures tell us Jesus grew in wisdom and stature as He grew in life.[10] This included an awareness of His heavenly Father. He became aware of His Father's indwelling heart, pleasure, and voice as He learned (as a man) to yield to all His Father revealed to Him. We can see the oneness of Jesus and the Father expressed in a few different areas.

ONENESS IN IDENTITY

In His prayer to the Father just before His murder, Jesus declares the essence of eternal life is knowing the Father, and His son Jesus Christ. As a human being, Jesus possessed this eternal life. He intimately knew His Father through His identity as the Son. Although this identity transcends time itself and is eternal, the scriptures tell us Jesus (in His humanity) needed to grow in His identity as a son through revelation.

At twelve years old, we know Jesus was beginning to become aware of the Lord as His Father. By the response He gave to His mother in the temple when they finally found Him there after a frantic three day search, we can see He was also beginning to identify with His heavenly Father's work over His earthly father's work.[11] This special relationship was also confirmed when the Father spoke before Jesus' baptism saying:

"You are my Son, whom I love; with you I am well pleased." **(MARK 1:11)**

Knowing God was His Father, and the Father *knowing* Jesus was His Son, seems to be a very significant element to their oneness. This *knowing* goes beyond an informational awareness and speaks to the depth of their relationship. Debra Hirsch, in her book Redeeming Sex, sheds light on this reality:

"The Hebrew word *yada* ("to know") is, in fact, used for both sexual intercourse as well as our relationship with God. *Yada* implies contact, intimacy and relation. It refers to both sexual intimacy in the narrowest sense of the word (in Adam *knowing* Eve) but also to our knowledge of God. This is significant: to *yada* God doesn't mean just having some abstract theoretical knowledge about God, but rather being connected to God".[12]

This special relationship was constantly under scrutiny by others who were threatened by its uniqueness. The way many of the respected religious leaders related to God was quite different; lacking the same intimacy and confidence Jesus seemed to have with His Father. For Jesus, knowing and treasuring the revelation of their shared identity was essential when tribulation and attacks against Him increased. In His identity as a Son, Jesus perfectly mirrored the identity of God as Father.

ONENESS IN WORDS AND COMMUNICATION

During His three-year public ministry on the earth, Jesus was continually talking and teaching about another world. Everyday life seemed to contain pictures and stories of what this new world was like. Again, the way He taught was different from the other 'spiritual' leaders of His day. Everyone could see that. He spoke with authority because the things He expressed didn't come from external sources of information. What He shared came directly from within. It was the overflow of what the Father gave Him.

Jesus was quite clear that His words came from His Father, and these words were given to Him because all the words that belonged to the Father was freely given to Him.[13] These words describe a reality that He knew intimately: the Kingdom of God that is alive and well within Him. It is in this reality that Jesus and the Father shared conversation and communion. Jesus' words and communication are a mirror of the Father's words and communication.

ONENESS IN PROXIMITY

Jesus had direct access to the Father's presence. He seemed to always be aware of Him. He spoke of His Father as if they saw each other continually. He spoke of His Father constantly, and when Jesus announced that He would be returning to His Father to prepare a place for them, His disciples begged Him to show them the Father.[14] They wanted to share the same space with the Father that Jesus seemed to share. Jesus' close proximity with His Father seemed exclusive and constant whether He was on a mountain in solitude and rest, or in the midst of the hustle and bustle of the crowds of people. The very existence of Jesus mirrored the oneness of God and mankind in proximity.

ONENESS IN RELATIONSHIPS

Jesus knew His disciples. Intimately. Although Jesus crossed paths with lots of people, He only had relationships with a handful. Like everything else, the relationships Jesus had did not originate with Him, but with His Father. The Father gave Jesus everything, and that includes relationships. Before Jesus died, He prayed for these relationships. In this prayer recorded in John 17, He indicates where these relationships came from.

"I have manifested Your name to the men whom *You gave Me* out of the world; they were *yours,* and *You gave* them to Me..." (JOHN 17:6, NASB, EMPHASIS MINE)

What would it be like to see our relationships in this way? To know we have a relationship with someone because they were specifically entrusted to us from our Father would cause us to treasure them immensely. We would be less likely to throw people away and cut them out of our lives if we saw people this way. So many relational storms could be weathered if we kept in mind where the relationship originated. We would carefully shepherd these relationships like gold. That's exactly what we see Jesus do with those given to Him.

As we can see, the oneness Jesus experienced with His Father touched every part of His life. By seeing that the Father shared *everything* with Jesus, hopefully we're beginning to get a picture of the nature and substance of what *oneness* actually is. For Jesus, sharing in His Father's identity, His words, His proximity and rest, and His relationships, was His very life. For the first time in human history, since the Garden of Eden, the nature of intimacy and oneness within the Godhead was now being expressed on the earth. This was the way it was always meant to be. But, that's only half the story. Oneness has more than a vertical expression. In actuality, the oneness of God is only fully manifested here on the earth through what I call *horizontal oneness.* We'll discuss that in more detail a bit later. God is love, and it is through the knowing and sharing of this love with one another that we can accurately recognize the oneness that exists between ourselves and others. As a result, we would do well to think about what it truly means to love another person.

AN UNEXPECTED HOME

Home is the center of our lives. We grow up, find love, and then pre-pare a new home where this love can dwell and expand. Growing up, I helped build many homes. After years of studying intricate building plans, and after each perfect stone discovered and laid in place, I real-ized there is something beautifully human about desiring and finding a home. Because we are carefully crafted together in the image and likeness of Father, when we express the essence of what it means to be human is when Father is displayed so majestically.

It is said that our father David was a man after Father's heart because he carried a true zeal for the house to be built. That same zeal is the substance of each beat that pulsates in my chest. The plans for this exquisite house have unfolded within me. They are precious. I carry them with me everywhere. I have left in search of this new home where my love can grow and multiply.

It was a tremendously long season. My friends and I had been to many places. My Father had so much for the people in those places on our journey. Such pain and anxiety in their eyes. They welcomed my gifts of love at first, but their fears often kept me at arm's distance. There seemed to be a shelf life everywhere I went, and I would leave with such unfulfilled desire and longing. Oh, if only they knew what I carried for them!

Where could I stay? Who would have all of me without shame? Some days I felt so tired, yet love propelled me dusty mile after dusty mile. As I sought a house for Father, I couldn't seem to find a place to lay my own head for very long. There always seemed to be something turning them away from me. Who would cherish and delight in me? Who would have all of me? No, these weren't questions I asked consciously. These were longings and groans within that came flooding to the surface the day I finally found a home. The day I laid my eyes on her is the day I found a home like none other.

As I spoke to the precious assembly of faces that had gathered in the village, I saw her. Oh, the delight in her eyes and her piercing gaze! She couldn't stop looking at me. Her eyes beamed with such beauty and light. Truth be told, I too couldn't stop looking at her. Her hunger for my words breathed fresh life into my spirit. As I spoke to the crowd, my eyes effortlessly kept finding her gaze. Looking into her eyes, I sensed warm waves capsizing over me, soothing me. Father hadn't sent me anyone like this before.

CHAPTER 6
AN UNDISSECTED LOVE

Many of us have said the words *I love you* to another person. When you say you love someone, what do you really mean by that? Are you speaking of the unconditional *agape* kind of love? Are you talking about the sibling kind of love expressed in *phileo* love? Do you mean something a bit more intimate like the love expressed through *eros?* Are you referring to a motherly/nurturing expression found in *storge* (store-gay) love?

If you are married or involved with someone romantically, *eros* love might be what you are most aware of. Eros is where the English word *erotic* is derived. The evangelical church world has limited eros love primarily to the sexual and romantic realm of relating. This is a monumental error for reasons that I'll explain. If you have a close, family-like relationship with a peer, you might think you love them with the sibling kind of love expressed through *phileo* love. If you are the type of person that loves humanity in general, you might think it is simply *agape* love in action. If you have a parental, physically nurturing type of love for another, you might think you are experiencing *storge* love.

While these examples of love may be examples of a*gape, phileo, eros,* and *storge,* it is a profound mistake to think these forms of love can be carved up and separated from one another exclusively. If you've spent any amount of time in the religious world, you know these forms of love are taught from a generalized generic standpoint and are understood as if they can be carved up and separated as stand-alone forms of love. This has caused tremendous confusion and fear in our relationships. God is love. More specifically, God is agape, God is phileo, God is storge, and yes, God is eros. God is all these expressions of love at the same time, and this love lives in you altogether at the same time. These expressions of love can no more be separated from one another than God can be cut up and dissected in His own person. As you love another person, all of these expressions of love will more than likely be present.

For example, let's say you are familiar and comfortable with the nature of *agape* love. You have a tendency to accept people unconditionally. As you generally see people as being made in the image and likeness of God, this loving disposition postures you to be accepting and open to others. This is the fertile ground where relationships can grow and develop. As you begin to form a relationship with another, you may begin to see them as family. You may even begin to experience a deep sibling (brotherly or sisterly) bond of *phileo* love for them.

As this relationship develops, you may also experience a strong and persistent awareness of them. Life without them becomes difficult to imagine. The more you are aware of them, the more your delight in them grows. This delight may also awaken a strong desire for you to know and connect with this person even more deeply. The desire for deep connection is the root of *eros* love. You may even have a desire for physical touch and nurturing to occur. The desire for some forms of physical touch can also be the nurturing expression of *storge* (parental) love. Yes, it is possible to experience all of these expressions of love in the *same relationship*.

It is very important we don't see these expressions of love as separate from one another. It is also important we don't box the expression of these forms of love into one type of expression only. For example, if we limit *eros* love (the desire to connect deeply and intimately) into the box of eroticism and sexual intercourse exclusively, things can get confusing quickly. The desire for intimate connection through sexual union is a legitimate longing and expression of eros love in marriage, but sexual union is not the only expression of eros. As a matter of fact, the act of sex is a very limited form of the expression of eros, but eros is actually involved in many of our relationships with people we are not married to. Because of our misunderstanding of this, whenever we begin to experience a strong desire for intimacy with another, fear enters the picture. This fear can be rooted in a variety of things, but a common fear is that becoming too close with someone will automatically lead to a sexual affair. This fear produces confusion, and ironically, it often leads to the very illicit sexual relationships that are feared. That's the nature of fear; it often becomes a self-fulfilling prophecy. This fear has also led to the justification of shallow and walled relationships as a protective reaction.

DAVID AND JONATHAN

We have a great picture of a relationship rooted in a multi-faceted love in the description of David and Jonathan's relationship found in the Old Testament books of first and second Samuel. People have speculated for years that David and Jonathan must have had a homosexual relationship because their love for one another seems to go beyond brotherly love (phileo), and into an intimacy that hints at eros as well. Here are a couple of passages that shine some light onto their relationship:

"Now it came about when he (David) had finished speaking to Saul, that the soul of Jonathan was *knit* to the soul of David, and Jonathan loved him as *himself.* Saul took him that day and did not let him return to his father's house. Then Jonathan made a covenant with David because he loved him as himself. Jonathan stripped himself of the robe that was on him and gave it to David, with his armor, including his sword and his bow and his belt." **(1 SAMUEL 18:1-4, EMPHASIS MINE)**

"I (David) am distressed for you, my brother Jonathan; You have been very pleasant to me. Your love to me was *more wonderful* than the love of women." **(2 SAMUEL 1:26, EMPHASIS MINE)**

These passages are a stunning description of a relationship that many have struggled to understand and explain. Jonathan and David were *'knit'* together from the very beginning. I love that the word *'knit'* is used to describe that Jonathan's soul was *knit* to David's. When two pieces of clothing are knit together, they become one.

For Jonathan, it was love at first sight. So much so, Jonathan gave David his most cherished possessions as a prince (his royal robe, belt, and weapon). He then made a covenant with David based on this love. This expression of love from Jonathan seemed to come first, before he and David had established a relationship. Jonathan simply loved him as his own being from the beginning. It wasn't rooted in David reciprocating that love, or history of friendship. It was there from the beginning, and Jonathan recognized and acted on that love.

This all-consuming love was the hallmark of their friendship. When Jonathan died, David wrote a song in which he described Jonathan's love as being more pleasant to him than even the typical romantic relationships he experienced with women. Although the *deep-calling-unto-deep*-type of eros love is certainly present in the love David and Jonathan shared with one another, those who try to pigeonhole this relationship into the erotic and sexual category miss the point entirely.

Many can't imagine a love greater than the sexual relationship pictured in romance and marriage, so Jonathan and David's relationship gets reduced into that category by some, and many others simply overlook it entirely. It is, however, an example of the kind of eternal relationships that are the very fabric of the body of Christ.

THE ETERNALITY OF LOVE

Did you know that the marital sexual relationship is only temporary? Jesus gave us a glimpse into the next age when He said marriage is not something we will experience in that realm. As a matter of fact, as our bodies age, the sexual intercourse dimension of eros begins slowing down and coming to an end naturally. Eros love, however, never ends. By His very nature as love (eros), God desires to know and be known intimately. This is the root of eros. God will love us with an eros expression in the kingdom of heaven, and we also will love one another with an eros expression in the kingdom of heaven. The imagery expressed throughout the New Testament of Christ being the bridegroom and we being His bride alludes to this type of love. Of course Christ fully dwells within our own being as well, so this type of interaction with Christ will not be disconnected from our interactions and relationships with one another. Amazingly, this new kingdom is breaking into the present, and that's why it's imperative we know this dimension of eros love in a way that is not limited to the sexual-romantic expression only.

Jesus is love personified. He is the first human being to love to the fullest extent possible. Jesus was not married, but He certainly didn't lack for the most intimate of relationships. Jesus loved others with *agape, philio, eros,* and *storge.* He loved fully. His love for others wasn't fragmented and dissected, and neither is His love in us. His new commandment for us to love one another in the exact same way that He loved is more profound than we have been told. Jesus shook the world by ushering in a new kingdom of love. Amazingly, He predicted that we'll go on to do even greater things. I'm guessing that has something to do with love as well. The question is...do we believe that our lives are capable of such a love?

"THE ONE WHO IS LIKE US MODELS A NEW WAY OF BEING HUMAN, OPENING UP NEW POSSIBILITIES OF BEING. NOW THAT WE KNOW HOW MUCH LIKE US HE IS, HE DEMONSTRATES WHAT GOD IMAGINES HUMANITY TO BE: SELF-GIVING LOVERS, JUST LIKE HIMSELF."

(ANDRE RABE)

CHAPTER 7
JAMAL, YOU'RE NOT JESUS

As I sat in my favorite little coffee shop in the Nashville, TN area, I was excited to have coffee with a friend to discuss my most recent blog post. I had just finished an interview on my blog about a thought provoking book: *Sacred Unions, Sacred Passions*[16], by Dan Brennan. It was one of the best books I had ever read about the necessity of cross-gender relationships. Dan's book challenged many of the religious and pop culture misconceptions about the dangers of friendship between men and women, and confirmed much of what I had been realizing about the nature of life in Christ.

In Christ, there is no Jew or Gentile, slave or free, male and female (Gal.3:28). We are truly one in Him. The revelation of humanity that Paul declares in his letter to the Galatians is more revolutionary than I had realized. These are all the distinctions that have kept humanity separated from one another since the great lie humanity bought into in the garden. In Christ, humanity is truly one.

The Jew/Gentile ethnic division was the first divide the church challenged and overcame in the first century, and it has continued to tackle ethnic divisions down through the ages. It continues to this very day in every culture. The church has also challenged the world's economic divides and the class systems that have kept people separated. Although the church has addressed these issues in various ways throughout the years, not many have dared to significantly address the entrenched relational gender divide that exists within the religious world. Dan's book was the first I had read that brought about reconciliation and the possibility of real friendship between male and female in a groundbreaking way. I had conducted a book review of Dan's book, and I also had him come on my blog to answer some questions. The dialogue was fascinating.

My friend (let's call him Bob) had also read the interview, and as I sat in that coffee shop with Bob, I could tell something was bothering him. After a few moments of awkwardly sipping our coffee and making small talk, he brought up the book review:

BOB: "Jamal, the things you have been writing about have some folks concerned".

ME: "Really? I haven't heard anything".

BOB: "Well, technically speaking, they told me they couldn't argue with the specifics of what you're saying, but they just feel like what you're saying is dangerous".

ME: "I'm simply advocating that we love people the same way Jesus loved people. He had no problem having intimate relationships with all kinds of people, including those of the opposite gender. Why is this so concerning?"

BOB: "Jamal, you're not Jesus. You have sinful flesh. He was different. In an ideal world, what you're saying would be great. The problem is, we're just not that spiritual".

With those words, a wave of nausea settled in the pit of my stomach. I realized the implications of what he was saying, and my heart was deeply grieved. Questions began to flood my mind:

- *What about the new commandment?*

- *Why would Jesus give us a command to love in the exact same way that He loved if it wasn't even possible?*

- *Did Jesus know He gave the radical command to love others the exact same way He loved to people who had fleshly bodies? What about the glorious mystery of Christ dwelling within us?* [17]

- *What about John's letter to the church which boldly proclaimed that as He (Jesus) is in the world, so are we?* [18]

I knew my friend was being held back by fear and was missing the point. I wanted to pose those questions back to him, but I was too grieved and shocked in the moment to respond. It was clear to me that Bob's questions were fueled by fear. He wasn't open to discussion and he felt he was doing his duty to address these concerns with me. Sadly, my friend's mindset is all too common among evangelicals.

My friend went on to tell me about the standards he has for his life. He has a rule of not meeting with females by himself, and he went on to defend his rules of gender segregation as a desire to protect the testimony of Christ. He suggested I might benefit from adopting these same rules, too.

After a few minutes, I simply told him that I would demonstrate the opposite of gender segregation in my relationships for the same reason he had cited: the testimony of Jesus Christ. I have never wavered in that commitment, and I hope I never will. My friend means well and is very intelligent. He truly wants to honor the Lord with his life, as do the many others who hold this line of thinking. I don't blame them at all. I just wish they could understand their self-imposed rules go directly against the grain of the new commandment to love as Jesus did.

How could my friend not see the damage that gender segregation has on the Lord's heart for oneness and shared life community? I'm convinced that until we understand and address the root of this kind of thinking, the assault on our identity, our ability to love, and on our relationships will only continue. So, what's the root of my friend's well-intentioned thinking?

REPACKAGED GNOSTICISM

The early church struggled with Gnosticism. The Apostles Paul and John specifically wrote letters to communities to address some of the errors that had been spreading into these communities, and sadly much gnostic thinking is alive and well in religious thought today. While there is a lot that could be said regarding Gnosticism, I would like to address a major component of gnostic thinking that negatively affects us today.

DUALISM

Gnosticism is rooted in an unhealthy form of dualism, a belief which makes an unhealthy distinction between the physical and the spiritual realms. Gnostic dualism regards the material world as inherently evil, and the spiritual realm as the only realm where goodness, purity, knowledge, and holiness can reside. By contrast, the natural world (including our created bodies) is regarded as impure and evil. This same kind of thinking forms the basis of a lot of evangelical and religious thinking when it comes to our natural lives in the flesh.

While the scriptures do draw a distinction between the spiritual and the natural in our lives , it does not demonize the natural (soul and body) components of our lives in the way many of us have been taught. When the Lord created us, He created us with a spirit, a soul (mind, will, and emotions), and a physical body. There is nothing inherently evil in the soul He created us with, nor is there anything inherently evil in the bodies He created us with.

Remember, the pinnacle of creation was mankind. After God created, He surveyed everything He magnificently made. Like a proud artist, He declared all of it as good. This includes our true identity as beings made in the image and likeness of God.

The problem with humanity came when they believed something false about their identity. They bought into the lie that they were not already like God, but could be if they acquired a special type of knowledge that God was keeping from them, even though the truth was that they were already created in His likeness, lacking nothing.

Humanity was always designed to live in union with the uncreated divine life of God (Tree of Life) from within themselves. In the description of the Garden of Eden, two trees are specifically mentioned; the tree of the knowledge of good and evil and the tree of life. Contained within the tree of life was the very eternal life of God that was freely available for mankind to consume. The spirit of mankind (united with the essence and life of God) was designed to influence our mind, will, emotions, and our bodies.[20] Our entire being (spirit, soul, and body) was created to be governed by and express the God who is love.

Instead, humanity violated their nature and allowed their natural mind (influenced by fear and lack) to govern their inner spiritual being where the Lord dwells. This propelled us to live in the fear and survival mode from which all sinful and rival-based behavior emanates. Again, the root of all sin is the lie of lack that assaults our identity.

Thankfully, Jesus is described as being the last Adam.[21] He is the true head of the human race. He was the first human being to live as humanity was designed to live. He was a human being like each one of us. His body and soul are like ours. This is why He could be tempted in the same way we are. The Word became flesh: not some different kind of flesh than we know, but the exact same flesh we have. Human.

- The Word became the same kind of flesh that gets tired, hungry, and thirsty.

- The Word became the same kind of flesh that urinates and has bowel movements.

- The Word became the same kind of flesh that gets irritable.

- The Word became the same kind of flesh that experiences sexual arousal.

We serve a God who isn't ashamed of our flesh in the least. He created the physical world and declared it good. He took on a physical body Himself, and lived and loved as a whole person, not just with a part of Himself. He loved with His spirit, His soul, and His body. The reason He could do this is because His soul and body lived fully integrated with His spirit where His Father dwells. As the true head of the human race, Jesus made a stunning declaration about the way we would now live:

> "Don't you believe that I am in the Father, and that the Father is in me? The words that I say to you I do not speak on my own authority. Rather it is the Father, living in me, who is doing His work...Very truly I tell you, whoever believes in me will do the works I have been doing, and they will do even greater things than these, because I am going to the Father...On that day you will realize that I am in my Father, and you are in Me and I am in you..." **(JOHN 14:10, 12, 20)**

We can love like Him. He is as human as we are. Jesus loved wholly. He wasn't trying to figure out what was from the 'spirit' so He could deny everything natural and physical in some gnostic way. The divine life and love from His Father dwelling in His spirit permeated *all* of His being. He loved with His spirit, His mind, His emotions, His will, and His body. His love was total and not fragmented. As He is in the world, so too are we.

With that said, it's obvious that we're all still growing in our understanding of what it means to be governed by love. That means mistakes will be made, and we'll learn from them. Believe it or not, Jesus Himself needed to *"grow in wisdom and stature"*.[22] The scriptures also describe Him as one who needed to *"learn obedience through suffering"*.[23] Obedience to what? To love. To the ways of love. Suffering and rejection taught Him how to hear the indwelling voice of His Father, the voice of love and fullness, in contrast to the voices of the world rooted in condemnation and lack. He had to figure this out the same way we do. If we truly realized how *human* He is, it would shock us.

Many people think they are making much of Christ by belittling humanity or by reminding others how much we're not like Him. Jesus did the exact opposite. He says *"I am the light of the world"*[24], and He also told His disciples *"You are the light of the world..."*[25] No separation. Just as Jesus said the things He did emanated from His Father and permeated through His own life, so the things that we will do should emanate from Him and permeate down through our lives, too. This is precisely why we can love exactly like Jesus did. Speaking of loving like Jesus, this opens up a wonderful new world of harmony and friendship between the genders that have been divided for a long time. My friend was flat out wrong. I am like Jesus, so are you, and this means *we can truly love like Him.*

THE INVITATION

*As the afternoon turned into evening, and as the people began to dis-
perse down the dusty roads into the sunset, I asked Father to keep
her near. I was compelled to meet her. As I blessed the people and
we exchanged our goodbyes, I kept her in the periphery of my sight.
My excitement began to build as I pondered the possibility she was
another special one the Father was giving me. I wasn't sure how far
she traveled, but unlike the others, she didn't seem to be in a hurry to
get home before nightfall. She was waiting for me, and I rejoiced with
Father in my heart.*

*Her smile welcomed me as I finally approached her. She seemed
uncommonly familiar to me and it brought a refreshing ease to my
heart.*

"Mary...my name is Mary, and it's an honor to finally meet you Rabbi".

*"And I you" I replied as I returned her warm smile. Her gentle, yet
dignified, strength shone. As I looked at her, I noticed something I
hadn't seen before in the others. Her eyes. She wasn't afraid to look
at me. Shame was absent from her gaze. Shame was so absent, it
kept her from feeling the need to separate from me. The others carried shame like a profession; constantly looking and pulling away.
Not so with Mary.*

"Where are you and your disciples staying tonight Rabbi?"

We accepted her generous invitation. The short walk to her home felt like a homecoming. When we arrived, Martha greeted us warmly. Never once did we feel we were imposing. Immediately, and with joy, Martha began to go to work on a lavish feast for my disciples and I. Martha was in her element, and it was easy to see! It was a sight to behold and soon the scent of a home cooked meal flooded the house.

I wanted to be near Mary. What she did next showed me she wanted to be with me too.

CHAPTER 8
THE LIE OF LACK

Humanity has been affected by a monumental lie. It's what I call the *lie of lack*. It's a lie that assaults our very being. It obstructs our view of oneness, produces an illusion of separation, and has caused a relational fracture in our relationship with God and others. The very root of this lie is illustrated by the first few chapters of Genesis in the story of Adam and Eve in the garden. Something was subtly suggested to them by the serpent: the notion that they lacked a special kind of knowledge necessary to be like God. To remedy this, they were offered fruit containing the knowledge of good and evil from the tree of knowledge.

The suggestion that humanity may not be like God deeply affected them. It was like a dagger that pierced the essence of their being. It was a lie that violated the very identity of humanity because male and female were already created in the image and likeness of God lacking nothing. The serpent was supremely crafty in making this suggestion.

There was nothing inherently enticing about the fruit of this tree until they believed it contained something they lacked in order to be who they were created to be. It was their perceived lack that made it desirable to their eyes. By taking the fruit of this tree, they were coming into agreement with the lie that stated they lacked something needed to fulfill the purpose of their existence; which is *to be the very image and likeness of God*.

Someone had to be blamed for the reason they didn't have what they needed. In this case, God was blamed. They began to see God as the one who kept from them what they needed. They began to see their creator as someone who was insecure; as someone who was afraid of mankind's potential to be like God. Mankind's desire to be like God (which they already were) then became twisted. They began to needlessly grasp—that is to say to lust—to be like God. This was the beginning of rivalry and competition.

The lie of lack was the beginning of a deadly cancer. It started very small and spread to each area of life; bringing death everywhere it lodged. It brought rivalry and death into their relationship with God, and then into their relationships with one another. The fear of not having what was necessary for life and survival brought the possibility of their own death into view. Because death was foreign to the true nature of God, it was foreign to the true nature of humanity as beings created in His image. Anything that goes against our natural created order brings about fear.

The fear of death radically shifted mankind's purpose from loving and multiplying (the garden), to an endless grasp to survive. It was a needless grasping, however. Although the lack was not real, their actions that emanated from belief in the illusion created real fractures in their relationship with God and one another. This had disastrous affects upon the earth they had dominion over. Within the lie of lack, human flourishing was no longer attainable: the best they could hope for was survival.

Immediately after accepting the lie of lack, they incorrectly assumed they were naked (lacking a suitable covering). In reality, their skin was their suitable covering. They were just as *naked* as everything else. This is why God asked them how they knew they were naked. He never told them they were naked as nakedness implies lack.

Nevertheless, the illusion of lacking a suitable covering brought about shame in their minds and led to their attempt to separate themselves from God's proximity. Their preoccupation became wrapped up in hiding and covering their shame. This is the fuel of human religion and effort. It's important to understand, however, He never separated Himself from them. It was Adam and Eve that hid themselves from God because of what they incorrectly assumed about Him. They imagined Him to be against them, which led to their adversarial stance toward Him. He never left or separated Himself from them however. Paul states in Colossians 1:21 that we were enemies of God *"in our minds"*. It's important to note that Paul states we were enemies of God in *our* mind, not God's. This is where humanity's evil behavior emanates from.

We, as humans, have been created with the inherit ability to live out and manifest what we believe on this planet. God is creative by nature, and as beings made in His image, so are we. As a result, when humanity began to believe they lacked something, the earth and the societies mankind built began to reflect this belief. Rivalry and violence are the creation of lives and societies built upon the lie of lack.

Although most people are not aware they possess this ability, God is aware. He created us with the double-edged sword of self-determination, and He allows us our choices. He never violates the freedom and authority with which we were created. If this freedom and authority were to be taken away, we would cease to be able to express His likeness and image that is the essence of our humanity. God is very passionate about our freedom and authority because it is only in this freedom and authority that we can fully love.

God is love, and we were created to be love's expression. When survival is our goal, however, it's impossible to see love. This is why Jesus said it is impossible to serve both God and money, which was made necessary because of lack. They are two very different pursuits. When Jesus entered the world, He came to demonstrate what God was truly like. Mankind's view of God was distorted as humanity projected their sense of insecurity (jealousy, violence, rivalry, etc...) into their view of God. Thankfully, Jesus demonstrated that God is not the bloodthirsty, violent God, the Jewish religious system made Him out to be.

To fully demonstrate what God is like, He would have to show us what it meant to be fully human. Jesus did not accept the lie of lack; therefore He was in rivalry with no one. He had nothing to prove. He had no ladder to climb. He was not afraid of death or lacking enough to survive. He was concerned solely with the business of love. Jesus existed the way we were always meant to exist. He loved, and He bore the fruit of love that multiplied on the earth. He perfectly bore the image and likeness of His Father.

It took a human being true to His own identity to demonstrate what God is like. When God became a human, He did not need to appeal to His divinity to demonstrate Godlikeness. To demonstrate true Godlikeness, He simply embraced His humanity. There was no grasping for what He didn't have because humanity lacks nothing in reality. Paul says it best here:

> "Have this attitude in yourselves which was also in Christ Jesus, who although He existed in the form of God, did not regard equality with God a thing to be *grasped,* but emptied Himself, taking the form of a bond servant, and being made in the likeness of men." (PHIL 2:5-7, NASB, EMPHASIS MINE)

For so long, I was told how unlike Jesus we are. Jesus was put up on an unreachable pedestal. As the Son of God, He was seen as completely 'other'. That's an unnecessary distortion. We are very much like Him. Although He is the Son of God in His divinity, our true identity is found in His humanity. I love that Paul encouraged us to have the exact same attitude as Christ Himself. That means *it is possible*.

Just as Christ didn't have to *grasp* to demonstrate Godlikeness, neither do we. We demonstrate what God is like by resting in our true humanity. Christ demonstrated what God was like by being made in the *'likeness of men'*. As human beings, we are the image and likeness of true love and we were created for such a mission. We lack nothing.

SIN…THE OFFSPRING OF LACK

It is in this context that we can understand what sin truly is. We've been told that humanity is inherently sinful. We've been sold a lie that our identity is tied to sin from the very beginning. That idea has more to do with the Roman Catholic concept of original sin than it does with what is communicated in the scriptures about our origins. Remember, the account of mankind's creation does not begin with their eating of the forbidden fruit of the tree of knowledge. Their beginning occurs before that, and God declares that His creation is resoundingly *good from the beginning.*[26] Let's be clear about something; there is nothing original about sin. Humanity gave birth to sin when we bought into the lie of lack. The lie of lack originates in the mind leading to twisted desire in our attempt to compensate for this perceived lack. *Desire* can come from lack, or from fullness. *Desire* itself is not the problem; it's what gives birth to the desire that determines its purity. It was *desire* that prompted the Lord to conceive you and give you life. His *desire* to create beings that can know and receive His love came from the over-flowing fullness of His being, not from loneliness or lack. He who is the fullness of love and life lacks nothing. It is the desire from love's fullness that gives us being, and this is the type of healthy desire we were created to have for one another. Desire from love's fullness is key to establishing and maintaining relational oneness with one another. When desire stems from lack, however, sin is not far behind.

What is stealing, murder, lust, or adultery after all? Do these actions not stem from desire rooted in lack and grasping? Again, these actions are an attempt to compensate from what is perceived to be lacking for survival as our greatest fear is the fear of death (the ultimate form of separation). The fact is, we were created by God and we were made for love. The illusion of separation from love and acceptance is detrimental to our being and is the reason why humanity has been driven by sinful desire in an attempt to compensate. Andre Rabe, in his book *Desire Found Me,* [27] says this:

> "We have seen how desire, born from a sense of insufficiency, can cause all kinds of destruction and evil. Even a desire for God can become deadly if its source is a sense of lack of being. In Jesus, God demonstrates again that He does not withhold anything from us, but freely gives Himself to us. He satisfies. Yet in this place of satisfaction, desire remains alive."

Again, Jesus was the first human being to live free from the lie of lack. He knew His identity and right standing before God. He was awake to the reality that humanity had been asleep to—the reality that mankind lacks nothing because mankind is not separate from the source of the fullness of love. We are not alone or cut off from God, even though we might sometimes feel utterly alone.

WHY HAVE YOU FORSAKEN ME?

Have you ever been in a difficult situation in which you felt others couldn't relate? It probably seemed quite lonely. Have you then met someone who went through something similar? If so, you probably sensed a measure of comfort. You may have felt your burden lift with this realization. In the same way, if you've been suffering under a specific hardship and someone came and put themselves in your situation and suffered alongside of you as if they were affected by the same tragedy, your sense of isolation probably significantly dissipated.

I have experienced this personally. I went through a season where little by little, most of my close friends began to see me through a lens of suspicion. My identity and character was called into question by a few who took issue with my views and embarked on a campaign to discredit me. During this time, many simply withdrew from me as if I no longer existed. The darkness and isolation that ensued was suffocating and torturous. It was a living hell that seemed unbearable and I despaired of life itself.

When I finally reached a breaking point, a few precious people came into my life and entered into the depths of that dark place alongside of me. Amazingly, they began to be affected with the same anguish and pain of loneliness I was feeling, as if they were being rejected as well. The more I became aware of their presence in my pain, the more I realized I really wasn't alone at all. The healing of that realization went deeper than I could have imagined and it pulled me out of a very deep and dark pit that I had tried and failed to climb out of myself. There is a reason for this. When we enter into another's burden, we are demonstrating that oneness is real and isolation and loneliness are an illusion. This is what God demonstrates to humanity through the life and death of Jesus.

Because of the lie of lack, humanity has been operating from an illusion of separation and isolation. As a result, mankind has lived as if they are separated from God and one another. This is the opposite of oneness. This has led to fear, shame, a sense of rejection, and loneliness. This is the root of sin.

Jesus took the root of sin into Himself. The scriptures tell us that Jesus *"who knew no sin became sin on our behalf"* (2 Cor. 5:21). This can be clearly seen through His words of anguish and despair when He cried out *"My God, My God, why have you forsaken me?"* Obviously, the Father did not forsake Jesus as love cannot forsake and remain love. The Father, who is perfect love, is incapable of separation.

Jesus was never alone or isolated from His Father as oneness is the essence of their being and personhood. The Father and Son are inseparable as a person. In the same way, mankind could not exist separate from the source of life. His being is the source of our being. In Him, all things consist and are actively held together as the scriptures tell us. Our very existence and life is a demonstration that separation is but an illusion.

When Jesus cried out on the cross in anguish and despair, He was joining mankind in the depths of their illusion of being rejected and alone. In this, the Father (through Jesus) was demonstrating that humanity is not alone or forsaken even in the midst of their deepest deception. Jesus entered our lie of separation and demonstrated in that hellish dark place where God is perceived to have forsaken us, that He (the fullness of God) is right there with us. By demonstrating Emmanuel (God with us), He exposed and destroyed the lie of separation at its very root. The more separation is exposed for the illusion it is, the more our eyes will be opened to the reality of oneness that exits between God and one another. *It is good news indeed.*

CHAPTER 9
WHAT ARE WE TRYING TO PROVE?

I'll never forget the time I attended a small rural church service to support my friend who was leading worship for them at the time. Their greeter realized I was not a familiar face, so he decided he would try to figure out who I was, and what I was doing there. After a few minutes of conversation, he asked me:

"Son, now tell me, how would you rate your marriage on a scale of one to ten?"

If you've spent any amount of time around the church world, you'll know that many ministries exist to help marriages survive. Many books have been written about how to better love our spouses, how to better relate to our spouses, how to avoid affairs, how to work through conflict, and every topic in-between.

In the evangelical world, it is understood that a person's marriage relationship is a barometer of their spirituality. For clergy, the status and condition of their marriages affect their qualification for ministry. This can be seen by the way spouses of clergy are scrutinized, or why Pastors often feel the need to physically objectify *(by saying "my wife is smoking hot" from the pulpit)* or celebrate their spouses publicly. When it comes to marriage in the evangelical world, it seems everyone is trying to 'prove' something either overtly, or covertly.

In the last twenty to thirty years, through the rise of ministries like *Promise Keepers, Focus On The Family,* and *Family Life Today,* to name but a few, much focus has been put on men to learn how to be better husbands and fathers in an attempt to rescue our society and halt the skyrocketing divorce rate. Women in the evangelical world have also been issued the burden of proving their spirituality by becoming the ultimate Proverbs 31 woman in which serving their husbands and children is the goal of their spirituality.

Somewhere along the way, it seems we've bought into the belief that the marital relationship is the closest expression of oneness and the nature of Christ's love on the earth. We have also bought into the belief that if we work really hard to have a great marriage, the world will know we belong to Jesus. We've heard it so much, it seems like truth. But is it?

In all honesty, I've never read anything like this in the New Testament. As a matter of fact, quite the opposite.

Contrary to popular opinion, Jesus didn't usher in a new kingdom for the purpose of improving our marriages. With the amount of striving the religious world puts into marriage, however, it would be natural to assume the marital relationship is the pinnacle of intimacy and oneness in the kingdom of God. Where did this come from? Could this have more to do with the romantic myth rooted in pop-psychology than the reality of the new covenant?

We no longer emphasize physical circumcision to point to the greater reality of circumcision of the heart, so why do so many keep the focus on the picture of oneness (marriage) when we have been freely given the reality of oneness?

While most give a theological head nod to Paul's declaration that the greatest mystery of oneness is the union between Christ and His church (Eph. 5:32), not many can tell you what that really means beyond the statement. I realize the questions I'm posing may seem to be demeaning toward marriage. Trust me, that is not my intention at all as I hope to further demonstrate throughout this book. Although these questions may be offensive to you, these are questions that deserve to be considered.

The deepest form of intimacy and connection we can experience with another is oneness. Our Lord longs for us to know, experience, and express the same oneness He and the Father share in our own lives and relationships. Before His crucifixion, Jesus expressed His desire for us to experience this oneness with one another in His prayer for us recorded in chapter 17 of John's gospel.

> "I pray that they will all be one, just as you and I are one—as you are in me, Father, and I am in you. And may they be in us so that the world will believe you sent me. I have given them the glory you gave me, so they may be one as we are one. I am in them and you are in me. May they experience such perfect unity that the world will know that you sent me and that you love them as much as you love me."
> (JOHN 17:21-23)

Jesus prays for a people to be as relationally one as He and the Father are. This oneness goes much beyond the watered down *"just getting along"* version of oneness and unity this passage is commonly associated with. The oneness that the Father and Son experience is deeply relational in its essence. Jesus envisions oneness between a people who are Jewish, gentile, rich, poor, educated, non-educated, male, female, single, and married. This oneness transcends all natural distinctions, including marriage. Of course He hasn't desired for us all to be married to each other, but He does desire that we would all experience oneness with one another. Our oneness with others is measured by the supernatural flow of the indwelling Spirit of God (love) within.

Contrary to popular opinion, the world will not know that we are expressing the character and nature of Christ solely by the way we conduct our marriages, but by the way we love one another through an intimate oneness that is not simply restricted to the temporary union of marriage, or any other distinction of our natural lives.

> "By this, all mankind will know that you are my disciples, if you have love for one another." (JOHN 13:35)

HUSBANDS LOVE YOUR WIVES LIKE CHRIST LOVED THE CHURCH

What about the teachings of Paul? Didn't he have a lot to say about husbands loving their wives as a special description of how Christ loves the church? What about Paul's statement in his letter to the Ephesians: *"Husbands, love your wives as Christ loved the church"*? [28]

If I had a dime for every time I've heard someone use this statement from Paul's letter to attempt to communicate that the husband/wife relationship communicates the mystery of Christ to the world in a greater way than other relationships, I'd be rich. Much of Paul's letters are treated in this kind of manner and it is truly unfortunate. Paul was writing a personal letter to the communities of believers in Ephesus that were experiencing a myriad of issues.

Like all of Paul's letters, they were written to address real problems communities were experiencing. Most who read the New Testament today are ignorant of these things and read these letters as if they are a collection of magical, stand alone, pithy statements that apply in a one size fits all type of way. This kind of erroneous thinking about the New Testament letters developed several hundred years after they were written and points to a much deeper problem regarding how we have been taught to understand these writings.

The community in Ephesus were facing some particular challenges. They were having issues with some groups of women who were using old mindsets and practices from their pagan religious backgrounds to subjugate men. Some men in the community were reacting to them in a harsh manner, creating family and household issues. Paul was writing to address some of these things and this is why he exhorts the men to love their wives and not treat them harshly.[29]

Remember the new commandment given to the disciples by Jesus? We are called to love one another in the exact same way that Christ loved. Paul is reminding husbands in that community of the new radical law of love that lays down its own life as the ultimate expression of love for another. He was reminding them that their wives are not excluded from this new law of extravagant love that applies to us all. Here are some questions we would do well to ask ourselves:

- *Who should we not love like Christ loved the church?*

- *Should parents love their children like Christ loved the church?*

- *Should wives love their husbands like Christ loved the church?*

- *Should brothers love their sisters like Christ loved the church?*

- *Should sisters love their brothers like Christ loved the church?*

The answer is yes. No one is outside of the boundaries of the new law of love. To take Paul's reminder to the husbands in that community and somehow suggest that it applies to them in a selective way was not Paul's intention. While the marital relationship is unique and sacred in its own rite, to suggest the marital relationship is on some sort of an upper rung in a perceived hierarchical ladder of relationships is simply not accurate.

Jesus never alluded to that at all. As a matter of fact, what Jesus did say about the natural family is quite destructive to the traditional nuclear family unit the religious world continually puts up on a pedestal.

He referred to His mother, brothers, and sisters in a way that had nothing to do with physical DNA. He also mentioned that the new age and kingdom we're heading into doesn't involve marriage. God's new Kingdom won't require any 'marriage ministries'.

It's truly unfortunate so many are desperately trying to prove to the world they love God through their marital performance as if it's some sort of a competition or question we have to answer. We're great lovers already as we've been created in the image and likeness of God, and His great commandment to us is that we, His beloved, were made and called to love Him fully through our love for one another. We can rest in this fact and simply express the love we already have to all the people in our lives, *including our spouses*. We lack nothing. We have nothing to prove, and everything to express.

CHAPTER 10
TOO MUCH LOVE AND INAPPROPRIATE ONENESS

Several years ago, I was asked to perform a marriage ceremony in which I would give a talk illustrating the love of God. I agreed to it without giving much thought about what exactly I would share. I loved the couple getting married and I wanted to serve them the best I could on their special day. After all, how hard could this be? Everyone knows that God loves us, right? I assumed I would give a standard little talk about love from 1 Corinthians 13 and tie that into the marriage of my friends. Nevertheless, I figured I would take some time and really pray about what I should share. Little did I know that what I would hear would change the course of my life.

INAPPROPRIATE ONENESS

Until that point in my life, I belonged to a stream of evangelicalism that emphasized that God was motivated by His own glory. In light of that, our life's goal was to simply decrease and get out of the way, so to speak. We would use the phrase *'it's all about Him, and not about us'*. Passages like Isaiah 42:8 were quoted often:

"I am the LORD, that is my name: and my glory I will not give to another..."

Simply put, the most precious thing to the Lord was His own glory. His glory was for Him, and strictly off limits to us. I had heard it so often that anything sounding as if God was motivated by the love and betterment of mankind was seen as spiritually misguided and dangerous. Much of my view of God was rooted in that foundational belief.

As the wedding approached, my friends wanted to know what I was going to be communicating in my message. A lot of their family and friends were going to be there and they wanted to have the peace of mind that I wasn't going to say something crazy as I was known to do from time to time.

They did, however, want me to speak from my heart. As a result, I began to press into the heart of God even more. I wanted to honor my friends and share what I sensed the Lord revealing to my heart for this momentous occasion. I didn't want to simply make it up. During my times of meditation and prayer, the gospel of John, chapter 17 kept coming to mind.

In this passage, Jesus is nearing the time of His crucifixion. The remaining time He has left on the earth is coming to an end, and He is beginning to summarize the last three years He's spent with His disciples. In this chapter, John records Jesus' conversation with His Father. As a son who had faithfully accomplished all His Father had asked of Him, He begins to recount the last three years of life with His friends. It's a beautiful conversation, but when Jesus recounts what He has given away to His friends, that's when I was totally caught off guard. This is what He said:

"I have given them the glory that you gave me, that they may be one as we are one." (JOHN 17:22)

For the first time in my life, the scandal of what Jesus was admitting to in that prayer became clear. Immediately upon reading this, the following conversation with the Lord ensued in my heart.

ME: Father, Jesus can't do that. That's not right.

FATHER: Why can't He?

ME: He can't give His friends (and us) glory because that is against your own rules. Remember, you spoke through Isaiah and said, "Your glory you would not give to another." I can understand that you would give Jesus glory because He is God, but we are not. How is it possible that He would share this most precious reality of yours with us? It's simply inappropriate. I understand He's excited and wants to share the best with us; but He can't share everything with us, can He? Where is the boundary or limit? When does the sharing become inappropriate?

FATHER: I understand your dilemma, but it's not a problem with me. You must not have heard the news.

ME: What news?

FATHER: The good news. I don't see any separation between you and my Son. When He gives you glory, He's keeping the glory in the family. The Bridegroom and bride being one is quite a mystery, is it not? Remember what Paul said:

"For this reason a man will leave his father and mother and be united to his wife, and the two will become one flesh. This is a profound mystery, but I am talking about Christ and the church." (Ephesians 5:31-32)

ME: Wow, I never thought of it like that.

FATHER: Until now.

ME: Wow, what a love we have been given!

FATHER: Exactly. Love is all we know. Love is the source of all creation. My glory is the expressed radiance of my love and no love will be withheld. There is no such thing as too much love. I love my Son fully, with all my love. That means I love you fully, with all my love. The same oneness I share with Him, We share with you as well. We are one.

It was oneness that allowed Jesus to give the love and glory of God to His friends, and it was oneness that allowed me to receive this love and glory. I find it interesting that I was realizing all of this as I was preparing for my friend's wedding. How appropriate. As Paul says, human marriage points to the greater mystery of oneness that exists within the community of relationships Christ is building in His body, the church.

I shared this revelation at the wedding, but the confused looks I received indicated that a oneness transcending human marriage is still very much a mystery two thousand years after Paul penned those words. Had my friends not given me the permission to share from my heart, I probably would not have been awakened to that discovery. I'm so glad they did.

THE MYTH OF EMOTIONAL ADULTERY AND THE REALITY OF THE NEW COMMANDMENT

Our deep desire for oneness makes up our DNA. Our Lord is one, and as beings created in His image and likeness, we are made to experience this oneness relationally. Unfortunately, a destructive lie pervades pop-culture. This same lie is the root of what much of what the religious world teaches about human marriage. This is the lie:

The marital relationship is the relationship where oneness is fully experienced. True oneness with another outside of the confines of marriage is not only inappropriate, but impossible.

Folks who have bought into this lie approach marriage looking for the intimacy of oneness. Once married, all other close and intimate non-familial relationships are usually dowsed with cold water. If those relationships survive, they are often a shell of what they used to be. Although what many call *emotional adultery* cannot be found anywhere in the scriptures, the fear of this invented offense is used to promote an unhealthy hierarchy of human relationships which see the marital relationship as the ultimate fulfillment of relational oneness. As a result, all other relationships must take a back seat to the marital relationship in order to protect the uniqueness of it. The belief in this lie has done considerable violence to the new commandment to love one another, and the essence of New Testament church life.

Please understand that I'm not minimizing the destructive nature of adultery. Also, when I state that emotional adultery is a myth, I am not speaking of the mental adultery that Jesus discussed in Matthew 5. There is no myth to that. Adultery is an illicit sexual relationship with someone who isn't your spouse, whether mental or physical. Being connected with another human being at an emotional level, however, is not adultery at all; rather, it can be something quite beautiful.

The point of Jesus' statements about adultery in Matthew 5 was to communicate that adultery is the same whether it is acted out physically or acted out in the mind. It all comes from the same root of *lack*. Lust is a form of 'grasping' from lack. It seeks to take from another to meet a perceived need. It's a perversion of a legitimate desire. It's a desire birthed from lack, not fullness. It exploits the one being lusted after and is the opposite of love.

The reason adultery (mental or physical) is so abhorrent is because it assaults our identity and the identity of others. It reinforces the lie of lack through its attempt to acquire and take in order to satisfy the 'self' that is grasping from lack. It also reduces the other human being, who is the object of adulterous lust, into an object to be exploited and taken from. In addition to that, mental and physical adultery communicates rejection to the spouse(s) of the unfaithful ones in addition to violating the uniqueness of the sexual nature of the marital relationship. This will be addressed further in the following chapters.

Love, however, is desire that flows from fullness (not lack). It seeks to serve and better the other. Love is not the absence of desire; it is simply desire that is the natural overflow of the fullness of love. It is a desire to heal and make the other whole. Even in the midst of delight and attraction, love seeks to express itself in a way that builds up. Lust, however, leaves its object empty and broken.

Many of us have been erroneously taught that becoming emotionally close to and loving another person who is not our spouse is akin to emotional infidelity. Not only is this pure fiction, this lie assaults our ability to live out the new and greatest commandment to love one another. While there is an eros (love) exclusivity between married couples, this does not dampen our ability to love other people in robust, emotionally connected relationships. Our love is not restricted to only our spouse.

In light of all of this, I have a few questions that I'd like to introduce to us at this point in our discussion...

- *When Jesus loved His disciples and friends, how much did He love them? Was His love generic and limited, or personal and intimate?*

- *When Jesus commanded us to love one another in the **same way** He loved us, did He intend for us to only love the same gender like that, or does He intend for us to love the opposite gender like that too?*

- *When Jesus commanded us to love one another in the same way He loved us, did He intend for us to only love a spouse this way and no other?*

- *Is it possible He intends for us to intimately and personally love others who we may not be married to in addition to our spouses?*

- *Does marriage restrict the application of the new commandment to love one another to our spouses only?*

- *When Jesus prayed for His disciples to be one in the same way He and the Father experience oneness, was He simply talking to people who are married to one another?*

- *Did He also intend for us to experience the intimacy of oneness with others we might not be married to?*

From strictly looking at religious culture, one might think Jesus said the following:

- Love only your spouse in the same way as I have loved you.

- If you are going to relationally love others who are not your spouse, make sure they are only the same gender as you.

- If you struggle with same sex attraction, relationally experiencing oneness and intimacy is only safe with the opposite gender.

- If you are married, make sure your relationships with those of the opposite gender are strictly superficial. Emphasize and define your relationship through protective boundaries. Love them in theory only, lest you commit the mysterious sin of emotional infidelity.

Obviously, Jesus never said anything of the sort. His heart in us is to love others in the exact same way He loved. He awakened us to this supernatural love—His love—which dwells within our innermost being. With this love, we have the ability to love others to the fullest extent possible. We can now have the same oneness with others that the Father and Son share together. This love drives out all fear, is extremely intimate, and transcends every possible natural distinction. This is how He loved, and this is our calling in the new kingdom He is ushering in.

As we come awake to heavenly love in us, it's more intimate than anything we have experienced. As the scriptures declare, it's only a revelation of perfect love that can drive out fear in us. Before fear can be driven out of our lives, however, it will first be identified and brought to the surface. Perfect love begins to penetrate and shake all the areas of our lives that have been affected by lies. The more we experience this divine love relationally with others, the more we will encounter fears we didn't even know existed inside of us. Lies and insecurities will come to the surface and will have to be dealt with in order for us to be able to move forward in our journey into this new kingdom of love. Thankfully, we don't do this alone. We take on these lies and insecurities with the patience and acceptance of those we are in relationship with. This is the nature of our healing.

This journey is not for the faint of heart, will be very costly, but is completely worth it. Again, patience is required both for ourselves and for those with whom we are in relationship. Part of loving one another is helping one another out of the prison of fear we've been trapped in our entire lives. Jesus, quoting the prophet Isaiah, said the Spirit of the Lord is upon Him to set the captives free. When we love one another intimately in relationship, this ministry of setting the captives free becomes our ministry as well.

MAY I SIT WITH YOU?

I love to sit. Especially after a long day. Most of all, I love to sit with others, relaxing with no agenda. I have found the best things in life flow out of those times. It's vulnerable, yet liberating, to be able to simply rest in our own skin. As our exquisite feast was being prepared, I sat in the community room to relax and enjoy the company of my disciples and the others from the village that came to join us for the evening. I loved the conversation that developed among us. We talked of the new kingdom, of life and love, and of course about the feast we could smell being prepared by the women!

Not all the women were off preparing the feast, however. Mary gently approached our room that happened to be filled entirely with men. It was not customary for women to sit with men in that room, and especially when a meal was being prepared. Mary was from a different world, however. I watched the eyes of the men widen in disbelief and horror as if they were witnessing a disembodied spirit enter the room. I have to admit, it caught me off guard as well.

The muscles in my face naturally stretched into a smile before I could grasp the enormity of the situation. Could this really be happening? Who was this woman of strength entering the room? Never, in all my life, had I witnessed an act of such courage. Again, I noticed her eyes. They were like the sea and I couldn't help but see the flame of my Father's light brightly burning from the depths of her. She didn't seem to notice the grimaces and looks of disdain on the faces of the men in the room. Again, her eyes were locked on mine as she gracefully made her way to the place my disciples and I were seated on the floor. She sat down with us as if she were born to sit there.

It happened in a matter of seconds, although it seemed time froze in honor of this momentous occasion. It was then I noticed I had stopped speaking in mid-sentence. The men's eyes shifted from Mary back to me, as if they were now waiting for me to address this taboo intrusion we all witnessed. I wanted to dance. Instead, I re-gathered my thoughts and kept my composure as I continued where I left off in our discussion.

Storm clouds began to gather in the heavens shortly after. Mary's freedom offended and made a mockery of a broken world built on the illusion of separation. Their best efforts to separate us would fail, however. Demands of pressing need and even the risk of offense to her own family would not shake her resolve to remain seated with me. All the words the Father gave me, she desired. There was nothing from the Father I couldn't give her. She was born to sit next to me in that place, and I would move heaven and earth to make sure this seat was not taken from her.

"I PRAY THAT THEY WILL ALL BE ONE, JUST AS YOU AND I ARE ONE—AS YOU ARE IN ME, FATHER, AND I AM IN YOU. AND MAY THEY BE IN US SO THAT THE WORLD WILL BELIEVE YOU SENT ME."

(JESUS CHRIST, JOHN 17:21, NLT)

CHAPTER 11
HORIZONTAL ONENESS

When we think of the Lord, it's appropriate to think of Him as a person, but not as an individual. His personhood can only be understood through a communion of relationships. By very nature and substance, God is love. Love can only be expressed when it has a recipient: it is essentially other-person centered. God, lacking nothing, has never lacked an object of His love. He has never lacked community. The Father, Son, and Spirit cannot function independently of one another. They each have purpose in one another.

The infinite reservoir of the Father's love finds a home and identity in the Son. The Son is the purpose and affection of the Father's love. In the same way, the Son finds His identity in His Sonship. It is His Father's love and desire for Him that gives His sonship identity and purpose. The Son loves the Father fully by resting in and receiving His Father's love.

When Jesus referred to Himself as the temple of God[30], and when Paul the apostle said God was pleased for all His fullness to dwell in the Son[31], there is a profound reason for this. By receiving His Father's love, the Father actually has a home and destination in the Son. This is where His love is able to fully rest and dwell.

Similarly, the Spirit finds her[32] purpose in taking the love and life proceeding from the Father and giving to the Son. It's impossible to think of the Father without the Son, and it is impossible to think of the Son without the Father. Without the Father and Son, the Spirit would also have no purpose. The Father, Son, and Spirit are intricately intertwined in purpose and passion.

The love that flows forth from the Father is immense. Because of the immensity of the Father's love, when the Spirit deposited this love in the Son, you and I were conceived to be the visible expression of this love. Just as the Son is the visible image and resting place of the Father, humanity was birthed to be the visible image and resting place of the Son. So, humanity is the final resting place for the fullness of God. Let that sink in for a minute.

The personhood and oneness of God is expressed through the relational love that is shared together by the Father, Son, and Spirit. In the same way, the personhood and oneness of God is made manifest on the earth as this love is shared within our own personhood.

DID YOU KNOW THAT YOU ARE A PERSON?

By person, I don't mean *individual,* I mean person in the same way that our Lord is a person. We were created in His image and likeness to express His personhood through oneness in a communion of relationships the way He does. This is why Jesus prayed we would be one in the same way He and the Father are one. You can't get more intimate than that.

In his book, *Desire Found Me,* Andre Rabe challenges the false belief of standalone individuality that pervades much of western thinking. As human beings made in the image of another, Rabe explains how single individuality violates the fundamental nature of what it means for us to be human:

"In other words, as a creature who reflects, there needs to be another besides myself to complete who I am. In this context the 'other' becomes an integral part of 'self'. There is otherness in me and part of me is in another. And the space between is not empty or stagnant but consists of a continual flow, an inexhaustible partaking of one another—the highest form of mimetic desire."

As a *person,* you are not an individual. You are a person comprised of a plurality of individuals.

Did you know those with whom you are *one* relationally are part of your very *person?* (Don't jump to the next sentence. Let that sink in for a minute.)

You are not alone.

You were made to experience divine oneness both vertically in spirit, and horizontally with other people. This oneness isn't something that needs to be established or accomplished by us. We are not lacking oneness. Oneness already exists and has been established before the foundations of the earth. As our eyes are opened, we simply discover this mysterious divine oneness that exists between ourselves and our Lord, and others.

Desire is key to recognizing oneness. Desire is a heavenly gift. Desire functions like our spiritual nerve endings. If we'll be sensitive to the desires of His life and love within us, we'll begin to become aware of those who are part of our person. Here are a few desires of oneness that I have discovered in my journey:

AWARENESS

A fundamental component of oneness is *awareness.* To desire someone is to begin to become *aware* of them at a deeper level. Whenever I become more deeply aware of another, that's usually an indicator of relational oneness. This awareness can manifest itself both consciously and unconsciously. For example, a few years ago I took a trip overseas for an extended period. It was a great trip, and I was enjoying my time there immensely. In the midst of the trip, I had a week from hell. I felt a deep internal grief that I simply could not understand. I felt like crying continually. Something seemed deeply wrong, but I couldn't identify it. The next week, someone dear to me from America was coming over to join me on the trip. By all accounts, I should have been looking forward to seeing her. Nevertheless, I suffered tremendously and mysteriously for that entire week.

The following week when my friend and her husband arrived, I was filled with joy to see them. Soon after their arrival, we went to a coffee shop to spend some time catching up. What my friend said to me completely stunned me. She told me the previous week was a week from hell for her. As a matter of fact, she told me it was one of the worst weeks of her life. I couldn't believe what I was hearing. Suddenly, I understood what was happening.

Although I knew we were connected in a significant way before, that event opened my eyes to the deep connection that exists in oneness. I realized I experienced what she experienced because we were experiencing oneness. The dimensions of the spiritual transcend space and natural knowledge. It didn't matter that we were on different sides of the world; nor did it matter that I was not aware she was having a difficult week. Empathy is becoming aware of another's plight and having a disposition of sympathy toward their situation. This experience, however, was much more than that. I experienced her pain as if it were happening to me personally.

Because of oneness, she is part of my 'person'. Oneness is the key to a shared life of joy and sorrow. As I shared the details of my previous week, it matched her experience entirely. That moment of realization was magical and sobering at the same time. We both realized we experienced that difficult week *together*, not separately. I was literally bearing her burden with her. It was not a conscious choice we made, but simply a state of our being. It gave me a greater understanding into the words of Paul from his letter to the Roman believers when he exhorted them to *"rejoice with those who rejoice, and mourn with those who mourn"*.[33] That experience helped me understand the nature of the desire my friend and I had been experiencing for one another. It was a sign of the oneness we share.

We are truly not alone. The reality of being spiritually aware of another to this degree is a beautiful mystery that we are all created to know intimately as a regular part of our lives. Realizing this dimension of oneness with another(s) changes our daily existence entirely.

DELIGHT

In order to *delight* in someone, you have to see the *light* in them. Although delight comes naturally to all of us, I believe delight is often misunderstood and confused for other forms of attraction. The root of delight *is* attraction, however. Love and light are very attractive. Why wouldn't they be? God is light and love, Christ is light and love personified, and humanity was created to be the full expression of light and love. When we truly delight in another, it's because we are attracted to the light and love we see in another. Attraction is absolutely nothing to be ashamed of.

Attraction is often equated with a desire for sex. While sexual desire is a legitimate expression of attraction, it is a mistake to think delight can only be expressed through sexual activity. There are many ways to embrace and express delight in one another. Failure to properly understand this causes many to fear and repress the holy delight we naturally see, feel, and carry for one another. Much of this is related to Sigmund Freud's idea of human relationships that have shaped pop culture as well as religious evangelical culture.

Sigmund Freud (1856-1939) is considered the father of modern psychology. In his ground breaking book, *Sacred Unions, Sacred Passions,* Dan Brennan writes about Freud's impact on modern ideas of relationships and human behavior:

> "Whatever opinions we have about Freud, there is no disputing that he put sexual energy squarely in the center of relationality and behavior. Freud attributed many physical behaviors to underlying sexual drives. He genitalized (sexualized) affection, physical tenderness, gestures, and desires even between brothers and sisters. Freud genitalized all sensuality—not just foreplay. He genitalized emotional closeness and depth". **(PP. 39)**

> "In the post Freud world, the romantic myth requires your spouse to be your best friend and requires that all others friendships be incidental". **(PP.43)**

Freud's sexualized views of all human relationships have largely been accepted by society and undergird many of the suspicions that evangelicals have purported about the dangers of intimate relationships outside of marriage. Sadly, Freud's views are widely accepted because of a vacuum of understanding of the all-encompassing nature of divine love. We'll discuss this more specifically a bit later.

I think it's important to note that true delight can only be sustained in an environment where there is an accurate view of humanity free from condemnation. Religious ideas about humanity's depravity have essentially blinded us to our true origins. Evangelicalism is one of the worst offenders. As we discussed earlier, humanity was created in the image and likeness of God. That's the essence of what it means to be human. We've never stopped being human, which means we've never stopped bearing the image and likeness of God. This is true despite the fact that humanity bought into a lie about themselves and about God in the Garden of Eden story recorded in Genesis. It was humanity that doubted their identity as the image and likeness bearers of God. God never doubted His own goodness and He never doubted mankind's true glorious identity as well. As Jared Gustafson says: *"When we changed our mind about God, He didn't have to change His mind about us. He's always had an accurate view."*

When the truth about humanity's nature sinks in, it changes everything. It causes us to see people and the light they naturally bear. This is true even if the people we see are in the dark about their own glorious identity and God's.

- This is why Jesus could look at the woman caught in adultery and see only a non-condemned woman worthy of being embraced.

- This is why Jesus could look at an emotionally extreme fisherman and call him a piece of the rock.

- This is how Jesus could look at Phillip and see a man completely without pretense or guile.

- This is how Jesus could look at Mary of Bethany as one who was not lazy and neglecting her sister, but as one who was undistracted in her devotion and love for Him.

Having an accurate view of humanity allows us to accept and delight in others in a world that often rejects and disdains people. *It shall not be so with us.* Although there are many misconceptions—and possible risks—regarding embracing and expressing delight in one another, learning how to recognize this innate delight we naturally have for others can greatly help us in our quest to recognize those with whom we have been destined to walk in relational oneness. Simply put, in whom do you delight?

PROXIMITY

If there is one thing the incarnation teaches us, it's this: *God wants to be with us.* Proximity. Contrary to what is commonly taught, the Lord's desire for Christ was not that He would be a sacrifice, but that He would have a body.[34] Why was taking on a physical body so important for our Lord?

For proximity.

Our Father had made His dwelling place fully in His Son. By His Son being incarnated in a body, they could be with those they loved in physical proximity. Have you ever been in love with someone? If so, you know quite well that you desire to be in proximity with those you love. Perceived distance is agonizing. After Jesus spent three years with His loved ones, He was getting ready to leave them for a brief period. His heart comes out beautifully in His conversation with the Father recorded in John 17:24:

> "Father, I want those you have given me to be with me where I am, and to see my glory, the glory you have given me because you loved me before the creation of the world".

The greatest human fear is the fear of being alone; and our deepest desire is to be in proximity with those we know and love dearly. This is consistent with His image and likeness. Whenever I sense a strong longing stir in me to be in closer proximity with someone, there's a good chance that relational oneness may exist and be developing with that person.

Best-selling author Bob Goff recently spoke at a conference where he talked about a very close friendship he had with a woman. The closer they grew relationally, the more he wished they lived in closer proximity with each other. When the home next to his became vacant, Bob got an idea. He talked to his wife about buying the home next door specifically so they could provide a place for his friend to live.

After he and his wife came to an agreement, they decided to buy the house. Bob then asked his friend if she would consider moving into the place next door so they could live life near one another. She said yes. Bob and his friend enjoyed a deep friendship in proximity with one another for the next ten years until she became terminally ill. When her illness progressed, Bob was there. Bob was there, tending to her as one needing hospice care needs help. He helped her prepare for death with dignity. Bob described those ten years of closeness with his friend as the best of his life. He loved the proximity, and he longs for that proximity again. What a day that will be.

SHARING

When oneness becomes a reality with someone, we will become aware of an overwhelming desire to share with them. We will desire to share our time, our money, our talents, our fears, our successes, our discoveries, our failures, and our secrets. We will have an overwhelming desire to share the essence of who we are and serve them with all we have acquired in life. This is a major way the family of God is joined together.

I have a couple of dear friends whom I cherish dearly; and some time ago, I had a strong desire to introduce them to one another. They both live in different parts of the country, but I longed for them to know each other. Because they are precious to me, I wanted to share with them what I treasured most—*themselves.*

When they finally met, they recognized each other as instant family. Seeing their delight in one another brought me such tremendous joy. I have seen this occur often. I'm convinced this is a very natural way the family of God comes together. We also see this in the way Jesus met His disciples and how He desired they know and love one another as well. This same desire, for the ones we love to love others we love, lives in us too.

In addition to sharing relationships, I have also discovered the joy of sharing the simple things in daily life with those I'm living in oneness with. I have one friend in particular with whom I love to share food. I love to cook with her. Simple things like picking things out at a grocery store and sharing in the food prep at home brings me an inexplicable heavenly delight. When we go out to eat we never order two entrees; just one, so that we can share. It's a joy to think about discovering a dish off the menu together and sharing it with her. As a matter of fact, it brings me such excitement that I've had to stop and think about why this simple action affects me so deeply. It has become clear to me that this simple joy and desire to share food with my dear friend points to a deeper oneness we share together.

In oneness, sharing becomes a joy, not a burden. Sharing in oneness becomes the very motivation of living and propels us forward in our journey of love. Sharing the essence of all that we have with others in oneness takes our love from invisible desire to visible reality. We simply desire to share life with those with whom we are one.

PURPOSE

Mark Twain famously said: "The two most important days in your life are the day you are born and the day you find out why". As we develop oneness with others, I have found we are left with a deep sense of purpose in loving them. Other things in life once considered important begin to seem trivial. All that matters is serving the person(s) you have been given to love. Laying down your life simply to demonstrate your love for them seems appropriate and even desirable. It's what many call the cross. Embracing the cross only makes sense as a demonstration of love.[35]

This kind of love feels like coming home to a place you've always belonged. Giving from the abundance of love in you for another leaves you with a deep satisfaction of knowing this is why you were placed on the earth. When the door is open in the other person to receive the love you have for them, it's truly the in-breaking of a future heavenly realm into the present. Jesus tells us this is a place of tremendous power and fruitfulness. When we abide in Him, we bear much fruit (John 15:5). Fruit is reproductive in nature as fruit contain seeds of new life for a new kingdom. It is love that draws out the reproductive seed from us (fruit) that leads to the expansion of the new kingdom.

Jesus goes on to tell us to remain in His love by keeping His commands (John 15:9-10). This might seem like conditional love until we grasp what His command really is. His command is to love one another and lay down our lives for one another as He did.

Simply put, His command is love, and we remain in love by continuing to love.

Many people are initially awakened to a deep love for one another, but staying in this love requires us to be in touch with a love that is greater than the offenses that are bound to come in any relationship of depth and interaction. There's no greater joy than when the one you love welcomes your love, and there's no greater sorrow than when the one you love isn't able to receive what you have for them. This is precisely why Jesus was described as being a man acquainted with grief: His love was seldom understood or received by those around Him. Love was all He knew, and all He desired.

The book of Ecclesiastes records Solomon's wise conclusions about life when he was well advanced in years. It took him most of his life to discover everything is meaningless in the end, except honoring God and keeping the commandments. Had he been awakened to the new commandment (loving one another), he would have said everything is meaningless except for love.

Again, oneness with others looks like being deeply aware of another, deeply delighting in another, desiring consistent proximity with another, sharing life with another, and recognizing your life's purpose is to love one another. If you're thinking this sounds a lot like marriage, *you're right*. But remember, marriage is just the shadow. Oneness is the reality.

"ONE WHO IS UNMARRIED IS CONCERNED ABOUT THE THINGS OF THE LORD, HOW HE MAY PLEASE THE LORD; BUT THE ONE WHO IS MARRIED IS CONCERNED ABOUT THE THINGS OF THE WORLD, HOW HE MAY PLEASE HIS WIFE, AND HIS INTERESTS ARE DIVIDED. THE WOMAN WHO IS UNMARRIED, AND THE VIRGIN, IS CONCERNED ABOUT THE THINGS OF THE LORD, THAT SHE MAY BE HOLY BOTH IN BODY AND SPIRIT; BUT ONE WHO IS MARRIED IS CONCERNED ABOUT THE THINGS OF THE WORLD, HOW SHE MAY PLEASE HER HUSBAND. THIS I SAY FOR YOUR OWN BENEFIT; NOT TO PUT A RESTRAINT UPON YOU, BUT TO PROMOTE WHAT IS APPROPRIATE AND TO SECURE UNDISTRACTED DEVOTION TO THE LORD."

(PAUL OF TARSUS)

CHAPTER 12
OLD WORLD MARRIAGE IN A NEW WORLD

Several years ago, I had a friend who we'll refer to as Zack who was full of life and zest. Zack was unique: unlike anyone else I knew. He loved God and others genuinely and passionately. He was creative, hardworking, and loved to travel the world. Many organizations sought to employ him. Some of those organizations even offered him six-figure salaries fresh out of college. Amazingly, he turned them all down knowing they would box him in and prevent him from being the person he was created to be. He was not your typical Christian. You couldn't put him in any box, although scores of well-meaning people tried unsuccessfully for years.

When Zack met the woman who would eventually become his wife, however, things began to change. At first glance, they seemed to have a lot in common as they were both creative types. Although they seemed to have the same interests, there was a difference. He had a passion for life, people, and the world, but she had an insatiable need for him. Shortly after their marriage, she began to feel jealous rivalry over the things many admired him for. Instead of being excited about his desire to travel, she saw it as something that took his attention away from her. Travel became miserable for him as his attention was divided.

While she once loved the way he loved others, she began to be threatened by his relationships and the time it took away from her. She questioned his motivation and involvement in the lives of others, and after a while, so did he. Spring and summer turned to winter in his soul, and it wasn't long before a blanket of snow fell on his heart and cooled his relationships significantly.

Zack also had a history of not being worried about money. He had a track record of not letting money make his decisions. He saw miracle after miracle sustain them and even propel them into the adventures the Lord had for them. When he wasn't worried about survival, he was continually reminded that they were well taken care of by their heavenly Daddy. He had incredible testimonies of God's provision and faithfulness over the years. His wife, on the other hand, worried a lot about how they would survive. Zack was told by the religious leaders in his life that it was his role as a husband to worry and carry the burden of survival for his family despite the fact Jesus said we are free from that curse (Matthew 6).

Zack knew his wife would not be pleased until he brought home a steady income from a stable company the way her father had done for their family. Seeing his wife worry so much about survival caused him to feel a tremendous amount of guilt. He continually felt like he was letting her down and was not fulfilling his role as a husband. It wasn't long before Zack began to take jobs he once loathed, seeking the security for his wife that she didn't know she already had. His magnetic personality and skill set acquired him a number of well-paying jobs, although they killed him on the inside. He traded the abundant life for an illusion of security time and time again.

Today, Zack has a stable life. It looks great on the outside, but on the inside, he barely has a pulse. He's a shell of the man he used to be, and was created to be. He has a lot of life and love to give, but he is divided. Like Paul said in the passage quoted above, my friend wants to love others with the love he has been awakened to, but he is also concerned about how to please his spouse. He has many troubles. Zack was once undistracted in his devotion to the Lord, but no more. I have personally seen this occur many times with numerous people, and it breaks my heart each time.

Zack has been taught this is what it looks like to *carry the cross* and love his wife, but I couldn't disagree more. My friend is a picture of what it looks like to be divided.

In any situation, if we try to mix the *old* with the *new,* we are going to have problems. Major ones. Jesus Himself said putting new wine into old wineskins would result in a broken wineskin and wasted wine. The old and the new are radically different. One gives way to the other. Marriage is a central part of our lives, and when a person who has been awakened to a new world tries to intimately operate with another who is still living in the shadows of the old, there will be division and troubles.

In the religious world of evangelical Christendom, most think that any two people who claim the name of Christ are automatically operating in the new world. This isn't necessarily true. The likelihood of someone immersed in a religious mindset operating in the shadows of the old world is pretty high due to the fact that evangelicalism has many roots in such thinking. According to the scriptures, those who live awake to the new world are rare in this age.[36] If you are awake to the nature of love and the new covenant, and you are in a marriage to someone who isn't, you are more than likely living a divided life.

SURVIVAL VS. LOVE

Those who live in the shadows of the old world come from a place of perceived lack and are living just to survive. By default, their lives are consumed with acquiring money, food, shelter, clothing, retirement, and other needs of survival. The pursuit of survival is the curse of the old world. While there is nothing inherently wrong with money, food, shelter, clothing, or retirement savings (they are gifts from God), we have been created to be consumed with something entirely greater than those things. Jesus expounds on this beautifully in the Sermon on the Mount as recorded in Matthew 6.

Unfortunately, most people (including Christians) needlessly live according to the pattern of the old world that is trapped in the prison of survival. Those who live in the reality of the new world, however, come from a place of inherited provision. They are no longer concerned with survival, but with love and the multiplication of love. They know all their needs hav e already been provided within the source of life.

Those who are still living according to the old world of lack will desire their spouse to share their burden to survive. As you can imagine, the spouse awake to the new world will now find this burden foreign and unnatural. Instead, they will be concerned with love and expressing the image and nature of Christ in their world, not simply survival.

However, the spouse still burdened by the curse of survival will often see the other spouse as being neglectful; feeling alone and abandoned in their burden to survive. This obviously brings conflict into the marriage, as the spouse burdened with survival demands the other to join them in their quest. If this occurs, the spouse awakened to the new kingdom of love becomes divided in their pursuit.

SEEKING LOVE OR EXPRESSING LOVE?

A love deficit is the ultimate hallmark of those living in the shackles of the old world as the old world is defined by the illusion of lack. Those who live in this illusion are in a desperate search not only to survive, but also to acquire love. In an *old world* marital relationship, the acquisition of love is sought primarily from the other spouse.

Those who are awake to the new world of love, however, are at rest from this quest to acquire love. Their pursuit is fundamentally different. They are awake to the abundance of indwelling love and life, and their pursuit is to share this love relationally with others. If one spouse is still operating in the old world of lack, however, the love expressed from their mate will never be adequate. They will be more aware of the love they believe they lack *from* their spouse, than the love they desire to express *to* their spouse. Also, the love their spouse expresses to others will be greatly resented. This will cause the spouse awake to the new world to feel further divided. Instead of being able to rest in a state of love, the spouse awake to the new world will feel a pull backward into the old world of lack in order to try to fill the other spouse's love vacuum.

Often, the spouse awake to the new will feel condemned and inadequate in their ability to love their spouse. While part of their awareness will be in the new kingdom, part of their awareness will be focused on the task of filling the other spouse's love vacuum. This division is very troublesome and difficult to carry. It is not the abundant life of the kingdom that Jesus said He came to bring us. This is precisely why Paul made these often-misunderstood statements about being divided in such a marriage:

"...Are you released from a wife? Do not seek a wife. But if you marry, you have not sinned; and if a virgin marries, she has not sinned. Yet such will have trouble in this life, and I am trying to spare you...But I want you to be free from concern. One who is unmarried is concerned about the things of the Lord, how he may please the Lord; but the one who is married is concerned about the things of the world, how he may please his wife, and his interests are divided. The woman who is unmarried, and the virgin, is concerned about the things of the Lord, that she may be holy both in body and spirit; but one who is married is concerned about the things of the world, how she may please her husband. This I say for your own benefit; not to put a restraint upon you, but to promote what is appropriate and to secure undistracted devotion to the Lord." **(1 COR. 7:27B-28, 32-35, NASB)**

Wow, can you believe Paul said this about marriage? This is truly a conversation from the New Testament that many conveniently ignore altogether. It certainly doesn't seem to fit the 'focus on the family' moniker of the religious world. The heart of what Paul is saying here is this:

"...yet such will have trouble in this life, and I am trying to spare you".

Living in two worlds is no fun. It sucks the marrow out of life. We were only created for one. However, it doesn't have to be like this. There is a better way.

I WANT YOU TO BE WHERE I AM

I marveled at her strength and love. Her love overcame all illusions of separation. In all of Israel, I had never seen anything like it. No one could have put up a wall that would have kept her from me. Not a room full of men, not the frantic demands of her sister, not even the rules of culture. Her love was blind to everything but me.

I loved to travel. I loved to deliver the much-awaited news of freedom to the people who had lived under oppression for so long. I loved to watch the load lift from their backs. There are no words to describe the joy of what it's like to see a face, weathered from years of stress and uncertainty, change before your eyes. To see their facial muscles relax, to see the corners of their mouths rise, to see their eyes widen in childlike excitement.

There isn't any place like home, however. No, I'm not speaking of Nazareth. I'm no longer welcome there. I'm speaking of Bethany. That's where Mary lives. Each time I left Bethany, I found myself long-ing for the next time I could come back. Mary made Bethany home for me. We were truly accepted there. Just because. No pretenses. No agendas.

Each time we left Bethany, after our many wonderful stays there, I could tell it became more difficult for Mary. It broke my heart too. It filled my heart with joy whenever she could travel with us, however.

Her love was fearless. We were family to her and she embraced us as such no matter what others assumed. The disapproving looks and insults from others had no quenching affect on her overwhelming love. When the crowds turned away, and even when confusion and fear paralyzed the hearts of the others, she could not be moved. Her love was a steadfast beacon of joy. As the darkest hour of judgment approached, I couldn't imagine enduring it apart from her love.

CHAPTER 13
HOPE WITHIN A DIVIDED MARRIAGE

When I think of marriages, I think of marriages in three groups. The first group of marriages can be classified as *divided*. Again, by 'divided', I mean one spouse is living awake to the new world of love and one spouse is still living in the old world of lack and survival. Another group of marriages can be classified as *worldly* marriages. A 'worldly' marriage is when both spouses are living in the old world of lack and survival. They both are preoccupied with career building, paying the bills, personal and marital development, and other stuff pertaining to survival. My personal view is that most 'Christian' marriages are in this category. A third (and much smaller) group of marriages can be classified as *new kingdom* marriages. This third category is thrilling.

Truth be told, just because marriages can be classified into three nice and distinct groups doesn't mean they fit into these three groups in such a neat and distinct way. Many marriages are in a transition of sorts; or will hopefully go through a transition into a higher revelation of love, but there are no guarantees. If you currently find yourself in a *divided* marriage, I want to speak to your situation and give you some hope.

DON'T BE AFRAID

I have found most of what is written or taught about marriage in the religious world is written from an undercurrent of fear; fear of adultery, fear of divorce, etc... Fear is the enemy of love, and so much of what is taught about marriage simply contributes to the problem in my opinion. For most spouses in a divided marriage, the one awake to the new world of love can be tempted to give in to fear because the spouse living from lack utilizes fear and accusation as tools of control. This fear manifests itself in two ways.

First, the spouse awakened to the new world is often made to feel like he or she is guilty of not truly loving their spouse due to the fact that they have a radically different way they view the world from that of their spouse. They have different priorities, and a different perspective. If one spouse isn't focused on filling the other's perceived love void, or if they aren't burdened with survival, they are made to feel they are not loving or being attentive to their spouse's needs and concerns. Because the spouse awakened to love is so passionate about loving, they can actually be susceptible to the fear of failing to love their spouse. Since love is their life's mission, the fear of failing at that mission seems unbearable.

Fear and love are opposites, however. Giving in to fear never leads to love. If you are in a divided marriage you have options. You could give in to this fear. You could try to focus on strictly pleasing your spouse in the name of loving your spouse. You could try to put your spouse 'first' in a hierarchy of sorts, thinking your performance in your marriage qualifies you or disqualifies you from being devoted to the work of the new kingdom. If you choose this route you have not sinned, but you will have lots of trouble as Paul said in his letter to the Corinthians. It never leads to real peace.

It's an illusion.

Giving in to this fear may indeed produce an illusion of peace on the surface, but in the end, the spouse awakened to a vision of the new world will grow tired trying to reconcile the world of illusion with the world of reality. The two cannot mix.

I recently had a conversation with a woman who was expressing concern about some of the writings on my blog. She made the assessment that some of the things I had written about relationships and marriage couldn't possibly be bearing good fruit due to the controversy and division it was stirring up among others. I reminded her of Jesus' own words:

"Do you think I came to bring peace on earth? No, I tell you, but division. From now on there will be five in one family divided against each other, three against two and two against three." **(LUKE 12:51-52, NIV)**

I find it interesting that Jesus said *"from now on"*. There is a reason He said *from now on*. Something had changed. A new kingdom is now breaking into this realm, and not everyone would be on the same page at the same time. The introduction of this new reality and kingdom will bring division. Jesus was speaking to a religious audience. Their families were all people who claimed to belong to the chosen people of God. The division occurred there, in their very own households. Why do we think it's different today? Doesn't *from now on* include today, too?

I asked her if she would consider Jesus' earthly life unfruitful because His teachings and actions also created controversy in families. I reminded her how Paul described spiritual fruit: *"...love, joy, peace, patience, kindness..."* Those are internal qualities we share with one another through relationship. Since this woman didn't know me personally, I asked if she was comfortable making the judgment that I was unfruitful; lacking joy, peace, patience, or kindness. I don't believe she is unique in the sentiment that equates division as unfruitfulness, however. It's a common misconception the religious community applies to marriages as well.

Most assume if a married couple is divided, something is very wrong. I have a different perspective. What if something is actually right? Why do we think Jesus' prediction about divided households doesn't apply to married couples? It is possible, and even probable, living a life awakened to the kingdom of love will bring division among families that claim to be walking with God. This was true when Jesus first spoke those words recorded in Luke 12, and I suspect it's still true today. It's not up to us to awaken another, including our spouse, to the new kingdom of love. We simply express the life and love we are experiencing to the best of our ability. We do this by continually remembering and declaring their worth, serving them where we can, and continuing to see them as precious gifts to us despite the division.

Recognizing that we're in a divided marriage is important. Being in a divided marriage doesn't mean we're failing to love our spouse. We can simply rest and accept what is. There is nothing more distracting to our vision of the new kingdom than trying to change our spouse, or feeling the need to please our unpleased spouse. Being free of this mindset is the best way to have an *undistracted devotion,* as Paul says, in the midst of a divided marriage. It's also the key to love. Love doesn't seek to change or control another person, nor does love require us to enter into the slavery and darkness we've been rescued from. It is for freedom that Christ has set us free.

The second way fear manifests in divided marriages is through the fear of loss. Much of what is taught about 'Christian' marriage is taught from a standpoint of avoiding infidelity and divorce. The possibility of infidelity or divorce can be a subtle and motivating fear that spouses can fall into. They fear that if they don't please their spouse adequately, they will lose their marriage altogether. Keeping the marriage together becomes the ultimate goal when such fear is present. Again, the loss of the marriage seems like an unbearable failure of love. However, the good news is that there is a goal that runs much higher than simply preventing divorce and infidelity.

SINGLE MINDED DEVOTION

If you find yourself in a divided marriage, you never have to be afraid of failing to fulfill your spouse's perceived love void. Their love void has already been filled; they just don't know it yet. It's simply your job to express the love that is already in you for your spouse and others, not convince them of it. Even though you may be married to someone who doesn't yet grasp the new kingdom of love and provision, you can still have a single minded devotion to the new world. Consider this statement from Paul, arguably one of the most mysterious and overlooked statements in all of the New Testament.

> "But this I say, brethren, the time has been shortened, so that from now on those who have wives should be as though they had none;"
> (1 COR. 7:29, NASB)

Say what, Paul? Did he really just say those who are married should live as though they weren't? Where are all the sermons and marriage books about that? I've brought this passage up with several people who have spent years reading and studying the bible. The most common response is *"Where is that?"* or *"Paul said that?"* After giving them the reference to the passage, they usually need to look it up on their own just to make sure I'm not making it up. Some go into great detail trying to explain what Paul didn't mean. Others, after reading it, often say this: *"Why have I never noticed this passage before?"*

That's a great question. Filters. We often don't see something because of a filter we've been operating from. We've been taught to see marriage as the highest and most intimate expression of oneness and love. Anything that doesn't support that mindset simply gets filtered out. Not only did Paul make this shocking statement, he actually meant something by it too.

When Paul said those who have spouses should live as if they didn't, he wasn't talking about abandonment. Love doesn't abandon others. Love doesn't kick others out. Love knows no separation. Paul wasn't saying married people should abandon their spouses. He also wasn't advocating married folks engage in extramarital romantic or sexual unions with others. That would deny the uniqueness of the marital relationship, and he was not advocating that at all.

The basis of living as if we didn't have a spouse needs to be understood in the context of the conversation of the passage. Paul was talking about not living a divided life; but a life of being awake to the new kingdom of love that is breaking into this realm. He talked about the benefits of being single in regards to being awake to this new world. Again, if we approach marriage through the old world mentality that is common, we will experience trouble and strife. Paul was speaking about a better way altogether. He was speaking about being undistracted in our vision of the new world of love regardless if we are single, or if we are married.

AN UNDISTRACTED IDENTITY

A friend of mine who we'll call Bethany attended a cookout in which two house church groups were meeting together for the first time. The groups had connected online, but this would be their first face to face interaction. Many of the people in the groups were married, but my friend was one of the few that wasn't. Immediately after arriving, she was introduced as the 'single sister'. Bethany was instantly irritated, but the more she thought about it, the more she realized exactly why it bothered her. Usually when people meet, they identify themselves by sharing their name not their marital status. After all, people are more than their marital status. This is more than simply semantics.

Bethany happened to be unmarried, but that was not her identity. She is a human being who carries the identity of Christ. She is an eternal being, as we all are. She was not happy that her entire personhood was being identified through the grid of her current marital status.

I think she has a really good point.

Many people see themselves as either 'single' or 'married' as an identity. This is unfortunate. Our marital status, whether single or married, is only temporary. When asked about marriage in the next age, Jesus shook the patriarchal paradigms of the religious community when He told them marriage wouldn't exist in the new era. Although we still live in an age in which people enjoy the gift of marriage, our identity is not tied to this temporary age. As eternal beings living in an eternal kingdom, our identity is not tied to anything with an expiration date. I believe this is the heart of what Paul was expressing when he made that controversial statement in 1 Cor. 7:29.

AN EXPIRATION DATE

Among the saints in Corinth, there were people who were married in the typical distracted manner that characterized modern relationships as well. It's interesting he says "the time has been shortened". What is he talking about? When something has an end, it means it's only temporary. Many people operate in this realm of time and space as if it's permanent reality. I don't know about you, but I wasn't born into this world thinking time would eventually come to an end. As a child, I assumed this world (and linear time itself) would continue on forever. This is the way the world thinks about our existence until we realize we've been living in an age that has an expiration date.

That was John the Baptist's message: repentance. Repentance literally means to have a change of mindset. He told the people their minds would have to change about everything because a heavenly kingdom, one that would have no expiration date, was just about to break in. Their previous ways of understanding reality would not allow them to see this new kingdom. When Jesus came on the scene, He began to proclaim this long awaited kingdom was here *now*. Nevertheless, many still didn't see this new kingdom Jesus proclaimed. Why? Yes, you guessed it. Filters.

Old mindsets act as filters that keep us blind to the new world that is breaking in all around us. The way we see ourselves, other people, and the way we understand family are the filters that keep us blind to this new world of love. The ability to love and experience oneness with others is only possible when we shed those filters and embrace an entirely new reality.

The arrival of this new kingdom in the present tense declares that the old order of things has come to an end. In the midst of an old world, we are now able to begin to live and express the essence of the new world. Being awake to this new world of love fundamentally changes how we understand marriage and how we function with our spouses. If you're reading this and you feel you're in a divided marriage, I want to encourage you.

You are free.

You are not being held hostage.

You lack nothing.

You are free to dive head first into this wonderful kingdom of love without distraction. You are free to love others from this undistracted place. This includes your spouse. The results of this are not determined by us, but the Lord. While I can't guarantee all your marital problems will end and you and your spouse will live happily ever after as a result of your decision to not live a divided life, I can assure you that you have nothing to fear. Love will sustain you in this new world.

"NOTHING IN LIFE IS TO BE FEARED, ONLY UNDERSTOOD."

(MADAM MARIE CURIE)

CHAPTER 14

DRIVING OUT FEAR

The opposite of love isn't hate, but fear. In my experience, the greatest obstacle that distorts and attacks relationships is fear. Religious fear is the worst offender. Most human behavior is a reaction to our own fears or the fears of others. As fear is eradicated from our motivations, the way we relate begins to change significantly.

John the apostle, known for his grasp of love, said it best when he said:

"There is no fear in love. But perfect love drives out fear." **(1 JOHN 4:18)**

This *driving out* of fear can be a violent process as there is a reason it has to be 'driven' out. Images of Jesus seeing and driving out the merchants from the temple come to mind. Just as the merchants didn't belong in the old covenant temple in Jerusalem, fear doesn't belong in us, the new covenant temple. It must be driven out by the force of love.

Before fear can be driven out, however, it must be seen and identified. It must first come to the surface to be dealt with. I have often wondered how love accomplishes this, but the more I have entered into intimate relationships with others, the more I have observed this process at work in my own life.

THE PRESENT TENSE OF 'I AM'

As God told Moses, His name is I AM, not I WAS, or I WILL BE. God is love and love transcends everything, including time itself. The past, present, and future are all now for God. He is the Alpha and Omega—the beginning and the end—and all the letters in between: He is omnipresent throughout time. This is why love is experienced in the present tense. We can observe this process at work in us when we begin to experience relational love. Show me someone who is comfortable being present with others, and I'll show you someone who is familiar with love.

Being present can be quite daunting a task. For many of us, it doesn't feel comfortable to simply be present. We usually don't realize this until we're forced into the present, and find ourselves squirming, or distracted. If we're running from something, if we fear the past or the future, or if we feel we lack something, those fears will come roaring to the surface in the present.

However, if we can learn to stay in the present and allow perfect love to bring these fears to the surface, healing can occur. Deep-seated fears that have been keeping us in life long bondage can be driven away once and for all. I experienced this for the first time just a few years ago.

As far back as I can remember, I've been afraid of something. Loss. As early as the age of six, I remember wondering how I could ever feel secure in life knowing the people I loved the most were eventually going to die. I was afraid of being orphaned and alone; convinced it was simply a matter of time before my worst fears were realized. I braced myself for bad news every time my mother went to the doctor, or every time she went to work when the roads were bad.

The anxiety I experienced as a child seemed suffocating and never ending. I eventually learned to shove this fear down into the inner closet of my heart so I could function. This fear would come roaring back from time to time throughout my teenage years, but for the most part, it was manageable.

When my daughter was born, and during the first few years of her life, I began to worry about losing her to an accident or some terminal disease. I worried that God might actually take my daughter from me in some twisted test of my devotion to Him. The terror of dread and loss I felt as a child came flooding back. Eventually, I learned how to lock it all away again.

One of the ways I managed this fear was through activity. I busied myself serving God, studying theology, planting a church, helping people, and traveling. While these things were not bad in themselves, they kept me busy from being at rest and present long enough to feel what was in my heart. I was afraid of being alone and orphaned, and the background noise helped distract me from that fear. I didn't fully realize how deep that fear went until I was awakened to a love that transcended every boundary and box in which I've seen it.

TWO DAUGHTERS

I remember the day my daughter was born. I was eighteen years old, and my world was spinning with everything from high elation to deep anxiety. I leaned forward in my chair with trepidation as the nurse handed me my own flesh and blood wrapped in a blanket. My eyes were drawn to her precious face, and I noticed something it took me years to put into words.

I was staring into the face of someone more familiar than anyone I had laid eyes on before. It was a subtle, yet striking similarity. A look. An expression on her forehead, from the top of her eyebrows to just below the hairline. I had never seen anything like it before on anyone. Except me. It was an image or likeness I noticed in myself, and it stunned me. Seeing this look and expression on my newborn daughter's face gave me the sensation of looking into a mirror. Realizing she came from my own body touched something deep in my being that I had no ability to process as an eighteen-year-old boy. Like most things that defy our paradigms, I shoved that memory away to the deep recesses of my memory. The sensation and realization, however, could never be forgotten. It came flooding back to me almost twenty years later.

When Jesus said we would receive more fathers and mothers, sons and daughters, and brothers and sisters here in this age than we would in our natural families (Matt 19:29), I thought it was a nice concept. I agreed with it in theory, but didn't know how significant the reality of this could be relationally.

I remember talking on the phone with a dear friend of mine who lived in a different city about her upcoming visit. She told me she had someone she was convinced I needed to meet. This person would be traveling with her, as part of a year of travel through the country. Wherever she sensed the Lord open a door for her to go, she went. They both wanted to come visit a church community I had been meeting with at the time, and I was happy to introduce them to my friends.

After they arrived, it wasn't long before I was sitting with our new friend, Emma, over a cup of coffee to get to know her better. It didn't take long for me to see that Emma was truly different. Refreshing. I understood why my friend wanted me to meet her. She seemed to have a great visit with all of us and she went on from there to the next city she was scheduled to visit for the next few months.

I left soon afterwards on an extended trip to Europe, and while there, I had a significant spiritual breakthrough. I could probably write an entire book about that experience.[37] In short, this awakening expanded my grasp of the love of God in a way I never knew possible. I experienced dimensions of His love as my own for the first time. My capacity to love others greatly expanded in a way I didn't quite grasp at the time. It was so profound and unprecedented it actually unsettled me. I knew someone who always liked to say that we are 'lovers in training'. Looking back on my time in Europe, I now understand that time to be part of my own training: a time to recognize and prepare for what was about to happen next.

Shortly after returning to the United States, I spoke at a small conference and shared the personal story about my experience and awakening to the love of God while in Europe. Amazingly, Emma was there in attendance. She, too, had experienced something quite similar, and my story resonated deeply with her. After a conversation with her, I knew she was the real reason I had attended that conference. Shortly after that conference, she ended her time of travel and relocated to my city. We began to walk in deep friendship and community with one another. We both had a sense of awe, and I realized we were experiencing a holy oneness that was from another world entirely.

One particular day a few months later, Emma and I were sitting at my kitchen table chatting. I don't remember the details, but at some point she said something that stopped me dead in my tracks. Emma said something that was phrased and said with a texture and tone I had never heard from anyone else before. That is, no one except myself. At that moment, everything faded away and a memory came rushing back to my mind of something I hadn't thought about in almost twenty years.

The image of my newborn daughter being handed to me twenty years earlier came rushing forth from the deep recesses of my consciousness. I remembered the scene of looking intently into her newborn face and noticing that look. That unique expression from the top of my daughter's eyebrows to the bottom of her hairline. The very expression and image that came from my own body. I remembered what it felt like to see an actual expression from my own body in another person. I was reliving that moment for the first time in twenty years as I sat there with Emma at my kitchen table.

What I saw in Emma was the same. It wasn't physical like my daughter twenty years earlier, however. It was deeply spiritual. It was as if I was getting a glimpse into her being. Of her spirit. What I saw in her was deeply familiar to me because I knew it was from my very own being. Instinctively, I knew she was a part of me. Somehow, in a deeply spiritual sense, I knew she came forth from me. I could feel it just as profoundly as I felt it with my natural born daughter twenty years earlier. It affected me deeply, but I didn't have the words to say anything in the moment. Looking back, I can see how that experience changed the dynamics of our relationship. I began to recognize her as a daughter. This experience also helped me understand some of the newly awakened parental feelings that I was experiencing. We eventually were able to talk about this experience, and it confirmed for her some similar things she was also experiencing regarding our relationship. Both the experience, and the conversation we had later, were holy and defining moments for us.

Previously, whenever I would hear someone speak of being a spiritual parent or having spiritual children, I would think of someone older having a 'mentoring' type of relationship with someone younger in a generic sense. Never in a million years did I think spiritual family was every bit as life altering and significant as physical family. I consider Emma a daughter in every sense of the word. I carried a deeply intimate and indescribable parental love for her. It was difficult for our own minds to grasp as it transcended anything we experienced before. This love was all consuming and left us in awe that such a love even existed. The scriptural term 'God is love' took on an entirely new meaning for me because of this experience. Everything else seemed to grow dim in comparison with this love.

As I settled into this love, something surprising happened. I found myself becoming more present than ever before. I also began to notice something else rise up in me that I hadn't experienced in a long time.

Fear.

Deep, paralyzing fear, coupled with anxiety. I had no idea where it was coming from, or why, but the fear and anxiety of loss seemed to grow greater and greater the more I embraced the divine love in me for this spiritual daughter of mine. I feared loss.

I feared for her safety on the roads in the same irrational way I feared I would lose my mother to a random car accident when I was a child. When she got sick, I worried it would be something serious or life threatening. It brought back memories of the fear I felt for my physical daughter when she was young. When others disagreed with or misinterpreted our relationship, I feared she would believe their assessments and reject me. I feared loss. It was irrational as all fear is.

Looking back, I realize this fear was nothing new. It had always been there. It was keeping me from being truly free to love throughout my life. My attempts to manage this fear kept walls up between myself and others. When love would take those walls down, my fears would prop them back up. I learned ways to live life in such a way that I didn't have to feel or face that fear. I stayed busy doing great things for the Lord. I loved and served people in a generic, relationally distant sense, but truly embracing perfect love for another and from another is what drives out all fear. As I mentioned, the process of perfect love driving out fear involves identifying the fear, bringing it to the surface in the present to be dealt with, and covering over the root of it with the truth of love.

PATIENCE

You know what's crazy? We can't do this on our own. It's a catch-22 of sorts. Fear destroys relationships, yet it takes the giving and receiving of love in relationship for fear to be driven out. See the dilemma? This is where patience becomes key. If a person remains in fear, it becomes a self-fulfilling prophecy. In science, Newton's Third Law demonstrates that every action produces an equal and opposite reaction. When fear is our focus, it causes actions that produce the very opposite of what we want. Ultimately, it takes a revelation of a greater love to the person trapped in fear to overcome their own cycle of torment and bondage. In a relationship, when one is gripped by fear, it is important for the other to lean into their indwelling love for the other to exercise patience. This patience will guard us from reacting to the fear-based behaviors in which our loved ones indulge. This patience is a tangible, healing fruit of love that often helps the other see their fear as the illusion it is.

For me, it has been the patient love of those with whom I'm walking in relationship that has overcome my debilitating fear of loss. I have another friend in particular who refused to react to my irrational fears of loss. She wouldn't coddle my fears by trying to demonstrate the opposite, neither did she withdraw from me. She just patiently remained with me without contempt or judgment. It was a healthy demonstration of acceptance.

As I began to see my fears weren't real, that I wasn't being abandoned or rejected, I sensed a new level of peace permeate into the deep places still untouched by love. It brought me to a place where I could identify the roots and origins of my fears of loss. It is in this place where perfect love began to drive out the debilitating fear of abandonment and loss that had tormented me throughout my life.

No amount of striving on my own could have driven this fear out. I needed perfect love to accomplish this. Although perfect love is an indwelling revelation, He has chosen us to be the expression and demonstration of perfect love to one another. Perfect love is relational by nature because God is relational by nature. The power we have to loosen the chains of fear from one another and to heal one another through perfect love is beyond our wildest imaginations.

FIRST SIGHT

It seemed fear was everywhere those days. We traveled by night and stayed hidden during the day. My friends were beside themselves. They feared for their safety. When I broke the news to them that we must go back for Lazarus' sake, they assumed death even though I reminded them it would not end in death. Not for him, and not even for me.

I didn't like what fear did to my friends. Self-preservation became their goal. People became objects to fear instead of children to love. A focus on survival and resources took center stage. I knew what was ahead. Their fear was taking its toll on me, too. I grew tired.

Seeing Mary so distraught over Lazarus pierced my heart. I would do anything to dry her precious tears. Father and I dreamed together what could be done. Seeing her rejoice at his newfound life was the drink of water I desired. I love to love her.

The brewing storm clouds were on my mind. I dreaded the days ahead. No one seemed to understand. No one except Mary. Mary dreamed of what could be done, rather than being stymied by what couldn't. She was blinded by love. She poured her entire inheritance over me without second thought to her own life. She seemed especially attuned to my state. She was the only one. The scandal it caused did not shake her. What a woman! What a gift!

The darkest days were approaching. The thought of her comforted me. She stayed with me. Her gaze never left me. I went to sleep determined she would be the first one I saw when love awoke me. Love brought me home.

CHAPTER 15
A NEW KINGDOM MARRIAGE

If you ask most self-professing Christians what the purpose of marriage is, you might hear something like this:

"The purpose of marriage is to demonstrate Christ's love for the church".

Or this:

"Marriage exists to be a demonstration of the same kind of oneness that the Lord desires with His bride".

Are these statements true? No, not really. Not in the way they are presented. They sound good but are often misleading and inaccurately used as standalone statements for the purpose of setting marriage on a pedestal that is inconsistent with the new covenant. Is a husband's love for his wife a demonstration of Christ's love for His church? Yes. So is a mother's love for her children. So is a father's love for his children. So is a brother's love for his sister. So is a sister's love for her brother. We talked about this in a bit more detail in chapter 9. To love one another in the same way Christ loves is the essence of the New Commandment; which applies in every relationship.

Many will argue that Christ's romantic nature as a bridegroom is chiefly expressed through the marriage relationship. Again, as a standalone statement, this is misleading. In chapter eight, we discussed the role *delight* plays in relationships. Delight is often confused as erotic desire due to the Freudian grid we have erroneously been taught to see relationships through.

There most certainly is a romantic element to delight, however, and that's why it is often misunderstood. This is unfortunate because delight is a very natural form of attraction that flows from love to all relationships regardless of gender. To equate delight and its romantic nature, with strictly a desire for sex is deeply damaging to the oneness the Lord desires to build among His people.

In regards to oneness, much has already been said. Oneness is the nature of how God relates with Himself within the trinity. This is love. As beings created to express the image and likeness of God, pursuing oneness in human relationships is the chief expression of love. Before the advent of Christ and the new kingdom, oneness was best *pictured* by marriage. In light of the new covenant that has come, oneness is now *experienced* through relational oneness itself.

The Lord desires that we would live in oneness with one another in the same deeply intimate way He and the Father live in oneness with each other. Of course, He has not desired us all to be married to one another. Oneness transcends the marriage relationship. It is a profound mistake to think marriage and oneness are the same thing. They are not.

There has been a lot of angst and disagreement by the evangelical religious community with the recent U.S. Supreme Court decision to legalize gay marriage. I find it interesting and ironic, however, that despite the disagreement about the decision itself, the religious community and the State seem to both have the same misguided mindset about marriage as being the highest expression of oneness. Supreme Court justice Anthony Kennedy said this when writing for the majority opinion in this case:

> "No union is more profound than marriage, for it embodies the highest ideals of love, fidelity, devotion, sacrifice and family. In forming a marital union, two people become something greater than once they were."
>
> **(JUSTICE ANTHONY KENNEDY, SUPREME COURT OF THE UNITED STATES)**

Again, marriage is a picture of oneness, but oneness itself is the reality. It seems both the religious community and the State are blind to this mystery. The advent of the new covenant requires us to see marriage through an entirely renewed mindset.

NO CONTRACT NEEDED FOR ONENESS

Deborah spent most of her thirties dating various men looking for the right 'fit' for a lifelong mate. She broke the hearts of many along the way, and had her own heart broken a few times as well. Eventually, Deborah began to develop a friendship with Mark, who became a spiritual father to her. He passed on to her rich things of the kingdom he had learned throughout life. She began to journey deeper with him in these things through their relationship. Mark loved her as his own daughter and she began to receive a father's love from him for the first time in her life. It was a love that her biological father hadn't been able to give her.

It is through this relationship that Deborah began to realize the depth of what Jesus promised us when He said we would receive fathers and mothers, sons and daughters, and brothers and sisters a hundredfold in this age (Mark 10:30). This relationship was unlike any other she experienced in the past. All other relationships had a temporary quality. Relationships she had within various religious groups and institutions she was previously a part of ended when she was no longer part of those groups. With the various men Deborah dated, those relationships ended when she (or they) determined they weren't attracted romantically anymore. The relationship with Mark was quite different.

True spiritual relationships are eternal. When oneness is experienced with a person in a relationship, they become part of you. Living life separate from them becomes unthinkable. A document or 'covenant' isn't needed to define a lifelong commitment to them any more than a parent needs a covenant to remain committed to their natural children. Seeing people as family changes everything. It is more than lip-service to call someone *brother* or *sister,* it describes a spiritual reality. We were made for family. We were made for deep, shared life relationships that are permanent.

Many people seek marriage in order to secure this kind of a permanent relationship, but as we all know too well, marriage commitments can be broken the same way dating relationships are broken. Family is always family, however. The key is actually seeing one another as literally being a part of the same family. The oneness we share with one another is eternal.

As Deborah's relationship with her spiritual father developed, she realized her desires for intimacy and oneness with another person were finding a satisfying and healthy expression. Without any effort on her part, her desire for marriage went away. Deborah had grown up imagining only one way that God could meet her relational desires, and yet God had surprised her with a familial intimacy she could not have imagined.

So, if it's possible to experience lifelong commitment and the deep intimacy of oneness outside the context of marriage, what then is the purpose of marriage in the new covenant?

THE MARRIAGE BED

What I'm going to say may sound disturbing to you, but it shouldn't. Paul was quite clear about why people should get married. With all the attention given to marriage in the religious system, you'd think Paul's reasoning about why people should marry would be presented in a more straightforward manner.

People should get married primarily if they have an over-whelming desire to have sex.

This might sound shallow and degrading toward marriage, but it isn't. A passion for sexual intimacy with another is a gift in the same way abstaining from sexual intercourse in singleness is also a gift. Sexual intercourse is a unique expression of love. Like all expressions of love, this expression of love desires to serve the other and have an outlet for expression. Paul says that it's better to express and fulfill sexual desire in marriage than to burn with unfulfilled sexual passion.

> "Yet I wish all men were even as I myself am. However each man has his own gift from God, one in this manner, and another in that. But I say to the unmarried and to widows that it is good for them if they remain even as I. But if they do not have self control, let them marry; for it is better to marry than to burn with passion." **(1 COR. 7:7-9)**

Again, Paul states it is better to remain unmarried than simply to marry for physical or romantic chemistry alone. But, it's quite clear that marriage remains in this age to give sexual passion and intimacy its proper expression. When this age comes to an end, and the new kingdom is fully ushered in, the marital/sexual aspect of relating will also end. In the meantime, we're living in a transition of sorts. The new kingdom has broken into this temporary age, and the marital/sexual picture of oneness still plays an important role.

THE PURPOSE OF SEXUAL INTERCOURSE

Sex remains important because it points to these greater realities.

1. Reproduction.

One of the more obvious functions of sex is reproduction. Life is precious and our Lord isn't done creating new expressions of His image and likeness upon the earth. Babies are gifts. The nature of physical reproduction points to a greater spiritual reality of reproduction, however.

Have you ever wondered why the Lord chose human reproduction to occur through the intimacy of physical union, the exchange of bodily fluids, and pleasure? It is a picture of the fruitfulness of spiritual reproduction. Think about it. You were conceived in the heart of God before the foundations of the world. You were conceived in the oneness and exchange of love between the Father, Son, and Spirit. Simply put, your being is the very offspring of love.

In the same way, Jesus said streams of living water would come forth from within those who have been awakened to Him. As we begin to relationally experience the intimacy and union of oneness with others in our lives, we share and deposit our reservoir of love (living water) from within us into those we love. The fruit of this sharing is an overflowing joy and peace that contain the seeds of reproduction of the new kingdom. These seeds of life cause the kingdom of God to be born and expand within others. The sexual and reproductive imagery in all of this is quite evident in my opinion.

I'm convinced when we love and experience oneness with others, it can affect more than just those with whom we're in relationship. Reproduction of the kingdom of God can extend to those we think have no connection to us as well. One unforgettable example of this comes to mind.

Several years ago, I met a precious woman named Cara who had encountered tremendous rejection and abuse. Her once tender and warm heart had become hardened and cold. Cara put up relational walls between God and others in order to protect her heart from further trauma. Despite my best efforts and those of others, nothing seemed to bring comfort or healing to her. A couple of years went by with almost no contact with her. During this same period, however, I was walking in a relationship with another person that was rich with oneness and Christ's love.

One evening on what seemed like a normal outing with this dear friend of mine, I remember experiencing something quite extraordinary. As we were spending time together, we both were overcome with an unexplainable delight for one another. We felt God's presence around us in a palpable way. It was a sense of awe that left us speechless. There were no words exchanged. Simply a gaze that lasted several hours. It was a holy moment that defied explanation.

Although I have long believed we are Christ's dwelling place and His literal expression to one another, I beheld the Lord's regal face in the eyes of my friend in a new way that night. As this was occurring, I remember the realization that I was born for that very moment. It was a feeling of home as the Lord was fully dwelling in our exchange. This might also sound strange, but I had the sensation something was cracking in the heavenly realms as we exchanged His love and delight with one another in silence. *It felt like the earth was going to break open.* I believed it was the chains of bondage breaking. My suspicions were soon confirmed.

Early that next morning, I received a barrage of texts from Cara, after nearly two years of silence. She told me of an encounter with the Lord that she had the night before. Many of the questions for which she had no answers had finally been answered. She realized how much she was loved and how present the Lord has been with her the entire time. She was healed in an instant. The two years of heartache had finally come to an end. She knew something new was being birthed in her.

Do you know when her healing encounter with the Lord occurred? Yes, that's right. It occurred the very night my friend and I were delighting in each other in that extraordinary way. I was stunned and I knew beyond a shadow of doubt the timing was no coincidence. I'm convinced the Lord was revealing to me the reproductive nature of walking in love and oneness with one another. The kingdom of God advances in this world riding the coattails of love.

2. Dissatisfaction

I'm convinced one of the main objectives of sex is not only pleasure and reproduction (which is important), but dissatisfaction. As pleasurable and fulfilling as sexual intercourse is created to be, it is also dissatisfying as well. I'm talking about a condition called 'post-coital tristesse'. This condition is a well-documented phenomenon that has historical references dating back to the Roman Empire. I believe post-coital tristesse is a fascinating experience that gives us a lot of insight into the human condition in general.

Post-coital tristesse is the momentary and fleeting sense of despair that often occurs just after an orgasm. It can last anywhere from a few seconds to several minutes. For fewer still, it can lead to hours of sadness or despair. This phenomenon affects both men and women alike, and people from many different socio-economic and religious backgrounds. It also affects people who have a history of satisfying, dissatisfying, and even traumatic relationships, leading many to speculate about the cause and root of PCT.

While I am not a fan of much of Sigmund Freud's ideas about relationships and humanity, I do find his speculation about PCT insightful. Columnist Daniel Woolfson, in his article about PCT, summarized Freud's understanding of sexual intercourse in this way:

> "(Sexual intercourse) was the closest someone could come to escaping the intrinsic isolation of human existence—by literally being inside

another person (or vice versa). So when sex is over, you can't help but realize that—as "together" as all the fondling, kissing, and mutual involuntary leg cramps might have made you feel—you're really always alone."

Freud was correct to assert that, as sexual beings, the root desire of our humanity is union with others. It is the opposite of isolation and loneliness. This is why Freud believed the desire for sex was all consuming. It is about more than simple pleasure.

The desire for the union and oneness with another—inherent with human existence—is not limited to sexual intercourse. The all too common assumption that bodily sexual union with another is the same as experiencing *oneness* with another leads to much disappointment and disillusionment. Anyone can have sex with another, but not all who are married and have sex experience the joy and mystery of the kind of oneness that Jesus prayed we would experience with one another in John 17:21.

- The union pictured within sexual intercourse has a beginning and an end, but the union expressed in oneness is timeless.

- The union pictured within sexual intercourse is confined to the marital relationship only, but the union expressed in oneness can be expressed in a plurality of intimate relationships.

- The union pictured within sexual intercourse is sustained by a limited reservoir of physical strength and supply, but the union expressed within oneness is sustained by an infinite spiritual reservoir of living water.

Simply put, the limitations of the sexual relationship show us of a desire to relate that transcends beyond the boundaries of sex and marriage.

A NEW COVENANT MARRIAGE

Paul told the Corinthian community it is better for people to marry and have sexual relations than it is to be distracted by unfulfilled sexual desire. He warns us, however, that marrying someone simply because of sexual desire and mutual romantic/physical chemistry will lead to a distracted life of trying to please both the Lord and your spouse. This will be a troubled life, and Paul goes on to say it's better to be single than to be divided in that way. He also describes singleness as a gift that only some people have.

So, what if you don't have the gift of singleness, and what if you have no desire to enter into the common marital relationship that is divided between trying to please your spouse and also being devoted to the kingdom of God? Is there anything else besides singleness or a divided marriage?

Yes!

With love, all things are possible. The highest state of being that Paul describes in his discourse from 1 Corinthians 7 is being undistracted in our devotion to the new kingdom of love. We know Paul thinks singleness is one way to be undistracted in our devotion to the Lord, but he also alludes to the possibility of being married and still undistracted in our devotion to the Lord. As I mentioned previously, this is an often overlooked statement made by Paul:

> "What I mean, brothers and sisters, is that the time is short. From now on those who have spouses should live as if they do not." (1 COR. 7:29)

The goal of Paul's entire discourse about marriage and singleness in 1 Corinthians 7 is for the purpose of securing our undistracted devotion to the Lord (1 Cor. 7:35). This, of course, should fill you with a lot of hope for your life in the new kingdom if you're single; but also if you're married.

If you are burning with sexual passion for another person and want to be married (or already are married) Paul's encouragement for those with spouses to live *"as if they do not"* is an indicator that it is now also possible to live in a marriage with an undistracted devotion to the Lord that was previously only limited to those who are single. Let's jump back into Deborah's story to see how this very thing unfolded with her.

The longing for relational oneness that Deborah previously associated only with marriage was now a part of her life as an unmarried person. She was content and very satisfied with the significant relationships (both male and female) that were given to her from the Lord. She had no desire for marriage.

Deborah is also a business savvy woman and came upon an opportunity to purchase a business. As she considered taking that step, she consulted with a man named Chris. Chris is someone who had become a good friend and spiritual brother to her. They both also recognized they were significant to one another. Both Deborah and Chris realized they shared similar vision and passions, so they decided to partner together in the business. He packed up all his belongings and moved across the country to her town to labor with her in this new adventure.

While some assumed their relationship to be romantic in nature, Deborah and her friend did not. They both deeply loved one another and were committed to one another for life as family in Christ, however. They both also knew of the significance of walking in oneness relationally and took that very seriously. Marriage and romance was simply not a part of the equation.

As time passed, however, a new dimension within their rich relationship began to open up. It was more than the attraction and delight for one another they already shared. This was different. They began to burn with passion. Sexual passion. For one another. It wasn't fleeting. As time went on, the sexual passion they burned with for one another only seemed to increase.

Again, they both were already committed to one another as family, so they didn't lack commitment. They also both realized the deep oneness and connection they shared with one another. That was not lacking. What they didn't have, however, was an outlet to express their sexual passion for one another.

Deborah told me had it not been for their sexual desire for one another, she would not have considered marriage with her friend. She was already committed to him as family. It was their mutual recognition of this burning desire that propelled them to recognize the Lord was bringing them together as husband and wife.

Deborah went on to tell me that her identity and focus in life didn't change with marriage. She doesn't see herself as a *married woman,* but a *woman who is married.* She had an undistracted devotion to the Lord as a woman who was not married, and she continues to have an undistracted devotion to the Lord during marriage. Deborah and her friend also already experienced relational oneness before they were married. The marital aspect of their relationship simply gave them a way to express the physical/sexual component of their relationship.

What's monumental about Deborah and her husband's relationship isn't the marriage they now have, it's the oneness they experienced before marriage, and continue to experience now in marriage. As we have said, marriage and oneness are not the same thing. Marriage is the picture, but oneness is the reality. A new covenant marriage is one where *both exist in harmony.*

CHAPTER 16
NAKED AND NOT ASHAMED

You have probably realized by now that this book was not meant to be about the glories and wonders of marriage. There are plenty of great books out there about that. I do, however, understand how someone reading this could conclude that I have a low view of marriage or that I believe it is simply a venue to have sex. While I do have a low view of the *type* of marriage often portrayed by our culture and religious system, I still believe marriage is a wonderful gift from God whose benefits include more than just sexual expression.

Marriage is a vital relationship here in this world that was meant to point to a reality beyond itself. While I do not intend to get into the depths and intricacies of the marital relationship, (as that would be a book in itself), I would be remiss if I didn't mention an aspect of the marital relationship (other than sex) that makes marriage an unique picture of the oneness that I have attempted to unveil here in this book.

NAKEDNESS
Like many people, I used to have a reoccurring dream of being *naked* in public. In my dream, I would have a shirt on, but nothing else. My most 'vulnerable' parts were on display for the world

to see, and I was terrified. To make matters worse, it was usually a place in which I saw people I knew.

Nakedness is a scary thing in this world of shame, condemnation, and ridicule. Nakedness is vulnerability. The lie that there is something fundamentally lacking in our being has made us ashamed of our nakedness. The story of Adam and Eve is a great example of this. The fact is, we were created *naked*. It's natural to be *naked*. It actually takes effort to be clothed and is a result of desiring to hide or protect ourselves. The more we are free of the lie about our identity that leads to shame, however, the more we will desire to return to our natural, *naked* state. The vulnerable posture of nakedness is where we can best love. It is a posture of openness and trust. Nakedness, however, is only a picture.

Please understand, I'm not advocating that we all abandon clothing and form some kind of global nudist colony. Human desire, both sexually and relationally, have been severely twisted as a result of the lie. We still live in a world that is affected by the lie. Because of this, Jesus was clear that our most precious treasures should not be casually "given to the swine" where they will trample over them and ourselves. One of the greatest treasures we can share with another person is the treasure of our self. To be practically exposed (naked) and given to another in this world requires a tremendous amount of trust and security.

In addition to trust and security, we currently live in a realm where space and time are limitations. This is one reason why I believe Jesus said marriage exists here in this age, but not in the next. While the spiritual reality of oneness that we have with others is not bound by space and time, the physical and practical expression of oneness that we are able to share with one another is. In addition to that, it is within the limits of this realm of space and time that the marital relationship was designed to be a special picture of this oneness here in this age.

Mankind is never alone, and the relationships we've been gifted with are a demonstration of Emmanuel (God with us). This is good news and is a demonstration that we are fully accepted.

In marriage, the demonstration that we are not alone carries into the most practical of our day to day realities. We eat with our spouses, we sleep with our spouses, and the practical daily necessities of life are shared with our spouses. In marriage, the other person sees us in our most vulnerable state. What we cover up to the world is revealed to our spouses. It is our spouses who see our nakedness and who accept our bulges, our warts, and all the little things the world sees as 'imperfections'.

Author and blogger Bronwyn Lea, addressing a question from one of her readers about the subject of nudity says this:

> "I do believe that in a sin-soaked world, dressing is the norm. However, we are still naked at times. The question is: when and with whom is it okay to be naked? As you have guessed, I think it depends on context. I think nakedness with our spouses is biblically celebrated. The things we cover for the rest of the world, we reveal to our spouses: exposing ourselves (in body and soul) to our spouses is a deep expression of intimacy...But when you and your hubby kick back to unwind after a long day: why not do it nude? There's something very precious about being able to recapture the "naked and not ashamed" status of the first couple from the very beginning."

What Bronwyn is saying here is quite profound. Being physically naked and unashamed with another person in marriage is about much more than just sex or physical nakedness. There is a safety and security about being able to share day to day life naked, unashamed, and fully given to another human being. The acceptance, vulnerability, and oneness pictured in the marital relationship with our spouse is a physical picture of the spiritual acceptance, vulnerability, and oneness we are destined to experience with others in the kingdom of God eternally.

A FAMILIAR VOICE

My eyes opened and my heart was pulsating with joy. There would be no more farewells. No more tearful partings to endure. No longer would anything stand in our way. When my eyes opened, I thought of her. I imagined her precious tear stained face turning to pure joy upon our first glance. Joy at the thought made me convulse with laughter. Morning light was breaking in and I knew she would be the first to come now that Sabbath and nightfall were over. It was a new day in every sense of the word. I waited just outside for her to arrive.

When I saw her coming from a distance, it took all my composure to remain from running to embrace her. She had to see for herself. For her sake. I wanted her to see the place of death that is forever empty. The minutes it took for her to arrive seemed like hours as anticipation filled each moment.

Predictably, she walked right past me. She didn't see me standing in the sunlight just outside the entrance to the cave. Her eyes, heavy with grief, were cast downward. She didn't see my love-saturated gaze. She was still seeing through a world tainted by death. My presence was simply not visible through her temporary lens. Those spectacles of death would be forever discarded in just a few moments, however.

When Mary came out of the cave, for the first time, I saw hopelessness and desperation in her eyes. She had made a pilgrimage to come see my body; a body that had been reduced to a relic of the life and love we shared. To Mary, all that was left of our love was a relic, and now, even this seemed missing to her. I couldn't endure seeing her in such agony. She approached me, pleading for me to tell her where I had taken the one she loved, and her name came springing forth from my mouth:

"Mary."

The sound of her name was precious to me. How I had often spoken that name to her tenderly in times of joy, in hardship, and through tears; Always to capture her attention and remind her of my presence and abiding love for her. Whenever I spoke her name, the tension in her eased and the muscles in her body relaxed. Her breathing slowed and deepened, and the anxiety fled.

This time, there was a delay and a look of astonishment mixed with unbelief. Then I saw her eyes open. Oh, those eyes. Those beautiful eyes. How I could dwell there forever. This was the moment creation had been crying out for.

CHAPTER 17
TRUST

Knowing how and who we trust is a significant litmus test of our spiritual health. In my experience, sharing life with people in relationship involves a tremendous amount of trust. This is true both in marriage, and in the intimate relationships in which we experience oneness. Trust is the ground we stand on. Without it, fear runs wild and eats away at the fabric of our relationships like cancer. Trust stands the test of time and prevents the Accuser from penetrating our vulnerable places. Unfortunately, the demonstration of trust in relationships is a rare thing.

So, why is it so difficult for us to trust one another? Where does mistrust come from? Those are important questions to consider. As Jesus said, the new kingdom of love is for children. Nowhere can this be seen more than in the way a child naturally trusts. While adults may dismiss children's simple naiveté, it was exactly this quality about children that Jesus cherished. I'm convinced a child's propensity to trust speaks powerfully about the natural state of humanity before fear enters the picture.

Children naturally assume the best and trust that every human being has loving and nurturing intentions toward them. Why wouldn't they? After all, they have been swaddled in a warm womb for nine months, nursed and cuddled after being born, fed, comforted, accepted, and magnificently delighted in by their family. It is only natural for them to assume of others what they have received in abundance.

Unfortunately, children have been born into a world created by a humanity that has bought into the lie of lack. This is a lie against our very being as it assumes our natural state of existence is lacking, and what is essential for life is limited in supply. Again, this lie runs deep and is at the root of every perverted desire and sinful behavior. When people (and the societies they build) operate from this place of lack, the awareness of lack and loss injects fear into the picture. This fear produces actions like hoarding, possessiveness, selfishness, jealousy, rivalry, suspicion, and eventually violence. It doesn't take long before the illusion of lack is suggested to the little children (often through hurt), corrupting them as it is received.

A major way this corruption is manifested in relationship is through a lack of trust. This lack of trust is often manifested through possessiveness. Possessiveness can be found in regards to anything we deem as essential for life, yet does not seem abundant in supply. When we are not aware of how fully we are loved, fear of loss is introduced into the way we view life. In response, we become possessive.

Nothing exposes our propensity toward possessiveness more, than when a plurality of relationships are involved in community. If we're going to be serious about pursuing a new covenant lifestyle of walking in oneness with others, however, the root behind a lack of trust will have to be addressed and healed. If you've been betrayed by those you've trusted in the past, lost someone close, or been abused by those you looked to for protection, you know all too well how difficult it can be to trust again. To trust others who haven't proved their trustworthiness seems naive, reckless, and even dangerous.

The problem is, when our trust is based in something external or something limited in supply, we will always find a reason to be afraid and to mistrust. Our trust must be rooted in the awareness of how fully we are loved. This awareness can only be found in the infinite supply of love from Christ that dwells within. That's when our trust becomes unshakable and is able to be extended to others effortlessly. This kind of trust radically changes the way we treat people in general and fosters the necessary atmosphere for love and relationships to flourish, a lesson I once learned in the most unlikely of places: a restaurant.

CASH AND I.O.U.'S ONLY

I spent several days in the city of Indianapolis some time ago and enjoyed lunch at Yatz: a popular Cajon food establishment known for their good food in the central Indiana area. As we walked into the restaurant, my friend commented,

"Oh, by the way, they only take cash or I.O.U. here".

Yeah right. I laughed at her. I've been to the occasional 'mom and pop' establishment that only takes cash (and this place was not one of those), but I've never heard of a place that takes 'I.O.U.'s. I checked my friend's information with one of the servers:

"Yup, cash and I.O.U.'s only".

What? What kind of a place gives out I.O.U.'s? I couldn't believe what I was hearing. I didn't have any cash on me, so an I.O.U. it was going to be. I felt extreme embarrassment as the man took our order and handed me an I.O.U. ticket for $12. As I stood there with my mouth hanging open in astonishment, he simply grinned at me and walked away. I could tell that he had seen that expression before.

As we sat down at a table to wait for our food, I couldn't believe what had just occurred. In an age where most people pay with credit or debit cards, establishments that only take cash usually have signs indicating as much. This was no mom 'n pop start up establishment: it was a well-established restaurant with several locations. They don't take credit/debit cards because they don't want to. It also seems that they want to catch their customers off guard by not letting them know about their cash only policy. It's like they *actually* want to give out I.O.U.'s to people. I've never seen anything like it from a business establishment.

When our food was brought out to us, I had a hard time tucking in to the plate of steaming jambalaya. My conscience was uneasy: was it right to eat this heaping plate of food I didn't have the ability to pay for? Fear and insecurity rose to the surface.

Love will do that: reveal fear and insecurity in places we didn't know still exist.

Again, before perfect love casts out fear, it first brings it to the surface. How did they know I was going to come back and pay them? They didn't know me; they had not asked to see my ID or driver's license. They had no guarantees, and yet they extended trust to me. To be extended trust based on credit or history of the past is one thing, to be extended trust with no external reason or strings attached is quite another.

As I sat there and pondered all of this, I sensed the Lord speaking to my heart. Here are some statements that I heard:

"My love trusts. My love believes all things".

"My trust of you is not rooted in you, rather, my trust is rooted in the source. I am the source and root of trust".

"Trust is a state of being".

"My trust is not naive or gullible because it is rooted internally in my own being and not in anything externally apart from me".

In that moment, Yatz was a small picture of what divine indwelling trust looks like. They extended radical trust toward their customers, not because of their behavior or history, but because of a culture of trust that came from within the restaurant itself.

Although my friend and I were only there for about 30-45 minutes, the culture of trust that existed within Yatz restaurant was palpable. It shook me deeply. This kind of a place didn't seem to fit within the world's economic system at all.

TRUST IS A REVELATION OF JESUS CHRIST.

Imagine for a moment a community of mothers and fathers, and brothers and sisters who radically trusted one another as a way of life and state of being. Imagine a lifestyle of trust that flowed from a revelation of Jesus Christ. Imagine the richness of relationships that could spring from a culture like this. The absence of fear that true indwelling trust brings would break the common familiar dams that keep us from deeply and intimately sharing life together in relationship with one another.

The good news is, we don't have to wait any longer to deeply trust each other. No, not because our trustworthiness is rooted in our history or behavior. The trust we extend to others is rooted in the infinite source of love that dwells within. It comes from the reality that we are infinitely loved. There will be no need to hoard our love from others, nor will we need to hoard those we love from others, when we realize the fullness of love that is ours continually.

Regardless if we are married or if we are walking in oneness with our family in Christ, we will need to draw from the infinite supply of trust within us to undo the ownership or possessiveness we may feel over those we love. It's easy to underestimate the authority we have as human beings. We have the authority to cultivate love into a flourishing relationship when we trust, and we have the authority to do considerable damage when we don't. Relationships rooted in a divine love for another are saturated in trust and have an enduring quality. This is precisely why Paul said this about the nature of love in 1 Corinthians 13:7:

"Love bears all things, believes all things, hopes all things, endures all things."

We can rest in the truth that each of our relationships are completely unique. No two are alike. We need not be jealous when someone we love loves another too, for we cannot be replaced. Love has no rivals, so we can celebrate the other relationships that our spouses and loved ones may have beyond ours. We can celebrate the life and joy those relationships bring to the ones we love. We can love without ownership and possessiveness because we lack no good thing.

To walk in this kind of trust with our spouses or deep friendships may seem unlikely or impossible in a plurality of close-knit relationships, but I can attest this becomes a way of life over time as we grasp the depth, breadth, height, and width of love that is continually ours. We have nothing to fear when we live from love. Greater is the love that dwells within than any external threat.

"LOVE BEARS UP UNDER EVERYTHING; BELIEVES THE BEST IN ALL; THERE IS NO LIMIT TO HER HOPE, AND NEVER WILL SHE FALL."

(1 COR. 13:7, ISV)

CHAPTER 18

THE BEGINNING

Congratulations are in order. You've officially made it to the beginning, and I've been praying for you. I've been praying for vision to see a new world of holy and scandalous freedom. We stand at the precipice of this vast world: the beginning of the great beyond. There is much to be explored and enjoyed in abundance. Don't be afraid to move forward. It may look treacherous at times, and it may look like all is lost. It never is.

YOU ARE FREE.

You are free to dwell in the house God is building for you.

No, this isn't a house you are building for Him as if He lacks a home. He lacks nothing. Neither do you. It doesn't matter where you live. You are free to see people, all people, as the very dwelling place of God.[38] You are free to delight in the image and likeness of God they naturally bear, even if they can't see it themselves. You are free to love and relate to both genders. You are free to discover the beautiful relational oneness that exists between you and others. You are free to love and intimately relate with others with the same limitless intimacy the Father and Son share with one another. You are free to follow Jesus' example of loving others in the same way He loved others, free of the religious rules of segregation and fear.

You are free to embrace your true identity.

You are like Jesus. Fully human. Fully capable of bearing the image and likeness of love. You lack nothing. You are one with the very person who is infinite love. Your very existence is rooted in His being. The only thing that has ever been wrong with you is the fact you have believed the lie that you lacked something that makes you the image and likeness of the perfect One in whose image you've been created. All the sinful actions you have ever engaged in find their root in that lie.

You are free to see marriage as a shadow pointing to the greater relational reality of oneness that transcends marriage.

You are free from seeing marriage as the top rung in a hierarchical ladder of relationships in potential competition with other relationships.

You are free to be undistracted to this new world of love.

If you are married, you are free to pursue this new world of love with an undistracted devotion. If you're in a divided marriage, you are free to love your spouse from the fullness of love you possess. You are free to resist the pull to enter back into the world of lack your spouse may be operating from. Drawing from Christ's infinite reserves, you are free to love your spouse with patience, despite misunderstanding, never rejecting or cutting them out of your life. Your awareness of the fullness of love has freed you from rejecting and separating from those who do not see what you see.

You are free to lay down your life as demonstration of the highest love.

Because you lack nothing, you are free from the religious mindset that seeks to *die to self* in order to attain something currently lacking. Instead, you are free to embrace the cross by laying down your life in service to the ones you have been given to love. You are free to patiently remain in love and walk in oneness with your loved ones as perfect love drives out the fears that have kept us in bondage.

You are free to live and love from a place of trust.

Because your trust comes from a place of infinite indwelling love and acceptance, you are free to resist the temptation to seek security in anything external. Instead of others earning a limited supply of your trust, you are free to generously extend trust to them based on your infinite indwelling resources.

You are free to keep the dialogue going.

When I first began to delve into the things discussed in this book, I was tempted to shut the conversation down because of the fears of others. We've all heard the horror stories of marital infidelity and unhealthy relationships. I was told on many occasions my discussion of this topic would lead to much confusion, sinful behavior, and heartache. I was warned about people to avoid and books not to read. I was told to keep my conversations about this topic private and advised to remove blog posts that were related to this discussion. I almost caved to this fear until I remembered something: *I am free.*

Not only am I free, so are you. We are a people after God's own heart. We've been created to passionately pursue the city whose maker and builder is God. This is a city built on a foundation of love that is held together by love. You and I, and the oneness expressed through our relationships, are an inseparable part of the fabric of this eternal city. I stand with you at the beginning of this journey of discovery.

If you've come this far in the journey, maybe you'll be willing to come just a few steps farther. I am not naive. I know the road ahead will be filled with uncertainty and potential pitfalls. There is much more to be discovered and shared, and many more questions to be answered. Yes, there are the tragic stories, *but there are the glorious ones, too*. We don't hear the glorious stories often enough. I want you to know that I am here ready to keep the dialogue going with you. I love to tell stories of love, and I have more stories to share. As a lover in training, I have made mistakes in my journey to love. You will too. I have learned difficult lessons along the way. My life is an open book and I'd be honored to share my experiences, the good, the bad, and the ugly with you if it would be helpful to you. If after reading this book you feel I could be of any assistance, please don't hesitate to give me a call or send me a text message: (614) 946-1960.

I would like to extend an invitation to you to join myself and others in a continuation of this vital conversation. For more information about the ongoing dialogue and how you can be a part of it, please visit www.freetolovebook.com.

THE EMBRACE

It was just the two of us. Together. In the garden. No more death and enmity to divide us. No more shame to hide from. Love had finally brought us back together. This was the moment we longed for. We were together again, and there was nothing left to separate us. The morning had come to replace the night, and our eyes were both opened. I am alive, she can see me, and there is no shame.

We embraced, and it was an embrace for the ages. My home is in that embrace. It always will be. As the embrace lingered, as her arms were wrapped around me, I sensed something in her. I sensed anxiety return to her. Fear that something would return to separate us again. Oh, how I wanted her to know that every obstacle had been overcome so we could be together. Nothing would come between us again.

My beloved began to cling to me in this fear, but I reminded her that she could release me. Rest. My beloved is mine, and there would never again be a night to replace this new day breaking in. This love is ours, and this love could never be contained. This love is returning to Papa, and this love must be proclaimed to the others until time and space are filled and reconciled to this love. Our love is your love, and it endures forever. We are forever one.

ENDNOTES

1. Young, William P., *Eve: A Novel*. Print.

   Eve is a masterpiece and a novel whose time has come. I highly recommend *Eve* to those who would like to take a fresh look at the creation story from Genesis 1-3 in a creative way that stays true to the text, yet looks beyond the myths this story is commonly understood through. It is a game-changer and an essential read.

2. Viola, Frank and Barna, George, *Pagan Christianity?: Exploring the Roots of Our Church Practices*. Carol Stream, IL: Barna, 2008. Print.

3. Viola, Frank, *Finding Organic Church: A Comprehensive Guide to Starting and Sustaining Authentic Christian Communities*. Colorado Springs, CO: David C. Cook, 2009. Print.

4. "By this everyone will know that you are my disciples, if you love one another". (John 13:35, NIV)

5. "Neither do people pour new wine into old wineskins. If they do, the skins will burst; the wine will run out and the wineskins will be ruined. No, they pour new wine into new wineskins, and both are preserved."(Matthew 9:17, NIV)

6. "A new command I give you: Love one another. As I have loved you, so you must love one another". (John 13:34, NIV)

   With this new command, Jesus unveils a new function for humanity. He described this function as being 'new' in nature because it is fundamentally different than the law based paradigm that the Jewish people had been operating from that had the purpose of restraining human behavior.

The call to love is 'new' because it is not a call to restrain and prevent, but for the first time in human history it's a call to deeply connect and give. The call to love unleashes humanity to its fullest potential as beings that have been created in the image and likeness of God (love).

7. "Yet a time is coming and has now come when the true worshipers will worship the Father in the Spirit and in truth, for they are the kind of worshipers the Father seeks". (John 4:23, NIV)

8. Many scholars believe Paul was either divorced or widowed at this point in his life. Prior to his conversion, Paul was a member of the sect of the Pharisees which required their members to be married.

9. John 17:21

10. Luke 2:52

11. Luke 2:49

12. Hirsch, Debra. *Redeeming Sex: Naked Conversations about Sexuality and Spirituality.* N.p.: n.p., n.d. Print.

13. John 12:49, 14:10, 17:8

14. John 14:1-8

15. Matthew 22:30, Mark 12:25

16. Brennan, Dan. *Sacred Unions, Sacred Passions: Engaging the Mystery of Friendship between Men and Women.* Elgin, IL: Faith Dance Pub., 2010. Print.

    Sacred Unions, Sacred Passions is a deeply riveting and compelling read about the possibilities of rich relationship between men and women. In his book, Dan examines how much of evangelical ideas and thoughts about the dangers of cross-gender relationships are not rooted in the teachings of Jesus or the New Testament, but in modern pop-psychology developed by Sigmund Freud. *Sacred Unions, Sacred Passions* makes a compelling argument, from church history, that deeply intimate and non-romantic relationships between men and women are possible and have always been a significant part of the Christian life.

17. Col. 1:27

18. 1 John 4:17

19. "For the word of God is alive and active. Sharper than any double-edged sword, it penetrates even to dividing soul and spirit, joints and marrow; it judges the thoughts and attitudes of the heart". (Hebrews 4:12, NIV)

20. Nee, Watchman. *The Breaking of the Outer Man and the Release of the Spirit.* Anaheim, CA: Living Stream Ministry, 1997. Print.

21. "The Scriptures tell us, "The first man, Adam, became a living person." But the last Adam—that is, Christ—is a life giving spirit." (1 Corinthians 15:45)

22. Luke 2:52

23. Hebrews 5:8

24. John 8:12

25. Matthew 5:14

26. "God saw all that He had made, and it was very good. And there was evening, and there was morning—the sixth day". (Genesis 1:31, NIV)

27. Rabe, André. *Desire Found Me: Exploring the Unconscious Movements of Desire - How They Form Us, Connect Us, Shape Our Greatest Ideas, Mold Our Societies, Influence Human History and Ultimately, How They Are Unveiled.* N.p.: n.p., n.d. Print.

28. Eph. 5:25

29. Without understanding the context of what was happening within the community of believers in Ephesus, it's difficult to understand what Paul was responding to in his letters to them and to Timothy who was there on Paul's behalf helping equip the church there. They were dealing with very specific issues as a result of the religious background that many of the believers came out of in that region. This led to problems between the genders. Because much of this context is not understood today, Paul's words are often used in a manner that is inconsistent with his intent and are used to promote the very gender divide that Paul consistently

spoke out against. An excellent resource that goes into much more detail about this is a book written by author Jon Zens titled: *What's with Paul and Women?: Unlocking the Cultural Background to 1 Timothy 2.* Lincoln, Neb.: Ekklesia, 2010. Print.

30. John 2:19

31. Col. 1:19, 2:9

32. The Hebrew word in the scriptures for the Spirit of God is *Ruach*. Ruach is a feminine noun that has been historically mistranslated into the masculine due to cultural and patriarchal bias. Many of the attributes of the Holy Spirit are typically feminine. For example, the Spirit of God gives us new birth (John 3:3), and is a comforter (John 14:26). Many modern scholars have attempted to address the feminine characteristics of God found in the Holy Spirit and draw attention to the fact that a feminine noun is used to identify the Spirit of God in the original Hebrew.

33. Romans 12:15

34. Hebrews 10:5

35. John 15:13

36. Matthew 7:14

37. In May and June of 2013, I had the opportunity to spend a couple of months in Europe. During my time there, I met a woman who was viewed there much the same way the Samaritan woman that Jesus encountered in John chapter 4 was viewed by her society. I began to experience a deep compassion and love for her that defied logic, as I did not know her. I began to perceive insights about her personal life that would typically be impossible for me to know. Her life was filled with a tumultuous history with men beginning with her own father. She had been wounded deeply and she didn't believe that 'a no strings attached' love existed, especially from a man. She could not accept that she was truly loved, and she was quite skeptical of my intentions. Nevertheless, I began to love her with an intensity and depth that I had never known before. I had no reference point for it. It was a new experience for me. I simply knew the love I was carrying for her was from a heavenly realm. I found myself awake at night weeping over her, and my spirit was often in deep awareness and anguish

over her. The love I carried for her was not romantic in nature, but it was no less intense. This love offended the religious sentiments of my own mind. As I wrestled with the Lord in much prayer about this, I began to have a deep abiding peace about what I was experiencing. I sensed the Lord encouraging me to trust the love He was revealing in me for her, and to be fearless in expressing this love. I was directed to John 4 and I was reminded that what was occurring in this situation was the same love that Jesus had for the Samaritan woman. Like the Samaritan woman, I was assured that the purity of this no strings attached love would be deeply healing and redeeming for her as it was for the Samaritan woman. I knew that I would see this resurrection of sorts with my own eyes during my time there. What I was experiencing was simply the same life of Christ that is described in John chapter 4 being lived out and expressed through me. Like the Samaritan woman, my friend wanted to argue with me about theological differences we had, and like Jesus, I simply wanted to talk about her and what her heart was longing to discover. Her hostility and deep pain had erected what seemed like impenetrable walls. After two months, however, I witnessed how the supernatural power of this love was able to transcend all the walls. I saw the exact moment when she finally realized that she was loved and I witnessed all her walls dissolve. I saw her eyes open to the reality of how much she is loved. It was as if scales fell off her eyes and she came undone. Through her brokenness and tears, I saw hope and light in her eyes for the first time and I knew she was healed and changed. Later that same day, I returned to the United States. This experience significantly altered me.

38. "In Him was life, and that life was the light of all mankind". (John 1:4, NIV) It is important to note that John carefully specifies in this passage that the life of Christ was also the life and light of *all* mankind, not simply 'some' of mankind.

Many voices. One message.

Quoir is a boutique publishing company
with a single message: Christ is all.
Our books explore both His
cosmic nature and corporate expression.

For more information, please visit
www.quoir.com

CPSIA information can be obtained
at www.ICGtesting.com
Printed in the USA
BVHW032321080720
583188BV00005B/560